Labor
Essays

1997

RENEWING AND
REVITALISING LABOR

EDITED BY
GARY
JUNGWIRTH

First published in 1997 by Pluto Press Australia Limited,
PO Box 199,
Leichhardt, NSW 2040
in association with the Australian Fabian Society (Inc.),
PO Box 2707X,
Melbourne, Vic 3001

Cover design: Trevor Hood

Index: Neale Towart

Typeset by Chapter 8, PO Box 687, Marrrickville, NSW 2204

Printed and bound by Southwood Press, 80 Chapel Street,
Marrickville, NSW 2204

Australian Cataloguing in Publication Data

Renewing and revitalizing Labor.

Includes index. ISBN 1 86403 035 6.

1. Australia. Parliament — Elections, 1996. 2. Australian Labor Party.
3. Australia — Politics and government — 1990-. I. Jungwirth, Gary.
II Australian Fabian Society. (Series: Labor essays (Sydney, NSW); 1997).

324.29407

Contents

About the Australian Fabian Society

The Fabian tradition is one of achieving social progress through research and education. Bernard Shaw and Sydney Webb began it in 1883, and generations of Fabians have placed its stamp on every facet of British and Australian society. Gough Whitlam adopted the Fabian approach from the day he entered Parliament, and the seminal 1972 Whitlam policy speech was a drawing together of the threads of twenty years of systematic Fabian research and planning. Arthur Calwell before him was always proud to call himself a Fabian, and tbe tradition has been carried on through Bill Hayden, Bob Hawke, John Bannon, John Cain, Neville Wran and Bob Carr. The present Leader of the British Labour Party, Tony Blair is a Fabian, as were, Neil Kinnock, Michael Foot, Harold Wilson, Hugh Gaitskell and Clement Attlee before him. Australia had its first Fabian Society as early as 1895, and 1947 saw the establishment of the Victorian Fabian Society, which became the Australian Fabian Society in 1984. The Australian Fabian Society is the largest Fabian body ever to exist outside Britain itself. It operates nationally, with members in every state and territory.

The Society has no policy beyond that implied in a general commitment to democratic socialism, and it issues its publications as the opinions of their authors and not of the organisation. It does not admit members of parties other than the ALP. Its aim is to promote education and discussion on policies designed to further the goals of democratic socialism.

If you believe that reason, education and ideas should play a larger part in Australian politics, if you care about the quality of the society we live in and the direction it is taking and if you share the ethic of democratic socialism, the Australian Fabian Society would welcome you as a member.

Gary Jungwirth
President
Australian Fabian Society
Box 2707X
GPO, Melbourne, 3001.

Introduction

The Australian Fabian Society has re-established the Labor Essays series established in 1980 and which ran for five years. The objective of Labor Essays is to stimulate creative thought within and outside the Labor Party and the Labor movement. These essays are a vehicle to assist communication and debate within the party and also between the party and the public.

The Australian Labor Party has always been the party with values, ideas and policies. Priorities change as society changes. Yesterday's issues and challenges are not the issues or challenges of tomorrow.

In opposition it is necessary to reflect, review and revise our policies and our programs. The period in opposition must be used fruitfully to renew and revitalise Labor.

Labor Essays 1997 are in the main papers presented at the Australian Fabian Society's Conference — Renewing and Revitalising Labor — which was held in Melbourne in July 1996. The aim of the Conference was to focus on the future — the rebuilding of the Labor Party and the review of policy — in order to enable the ALP to return to government within a term.

Obviously after thirteen consecutive years of Government an election loss is devestating. The art of opposition must be quickly relearnt.

Many of the papers place emphasis on a return to core values — equity, justice and fairness. Their is also a recognition that the ALP must regain the votes of its heartland — the traditional supporters who deserted Labor.

The papers by Barry Jones and Gary Gray are brutally honest and frank assessments of the 1996 election loss and clearly outline what went wrong and why it went wrong. But both papers also address the priorities for the future.

The next two papers are contributions by Gareth Evans and Kim Beazley and concern the economic fundamentals. Gareth Evans outlines the prorities for our economic policies while Kim Beazley's paper was his strong response to the budget.

The papers by Mark Latham, Lindsay Tanner and Martin Ferguson are well argued papers on Labor values and policy priorities by three of our most talented new members of the front bench.

Neil O'Keefe also puts a strong case for simple focussed themes in order to communicate to the electorate. He also outlines the key issues facing his shadow portfolio. John Brumby outlines the challenges facing the ALP in Victoria as it prepares to regain the trust and support of the electorate.

The last series of Labor Essays was intended to last forever. No such claim will be made this time! But it is the intention of the Australian Fabian Society to continue to publish this series for a long time as practically all significant economic, environmental and social reforms are as a result of Labor initiatives. Labor Essays will provide an avenue to outline new advances in policy which will form the backbone for our programs in our next term in office.

Gary Jungwirth
President Australian Fabian Society

Contributors

Barry Jones   National President of the Australian Labor Party and previously Minister for Science 1983–1990.

Gary Gray   National Secretary of the Australian Labor Party.

Gareth Evans   Deputy Leader of the Opposition and Shadow Treasurer. Minister in Hawke and Keating Governments.

Kim Beazley   Leader of the Opposition and Minister in Hawke and Keating Governments.

Mark Latham   Shadow Minister for Competition Policy and Shadow Minister for Local Government. Former Councillor and Mayor of Liverpool.

Lindsay Tanner   Shadow Minister for Transport. Former State Secretary Federated Clerks Union.

Martin Ferguson   Shadow Minister for Employment and Training. Former President of the ACTU.

Neil O'Keefe   Shadow Minister for Resources and Energy.

John Brumby   Leader of the Opposition (Victoria) and former Federal Member for Bendigo.

Editor

Gary Jungwirth   President of the Australian Fabian Society. Former Councillor and Mayor City of Preston.

Chapter 1

Notes on the Election Defeat

Barry Jones

Exit polling conducted for the ALP by UMR Research Pty Ltd on 2 March 1996 indicated a swing to Labor of 3 per cent, and a swing against of 9 per cent, a net loss of 6 per cent. Nine per cent of voters claimed to have made up their minds on polling day.

The exit polling indicated a spectacular drop in Labor's vote by people whose household income was less than $20 000. If families were hurting badly, who else could they blame? Among those with household incomes of $50–60 000 Labor's vote (while still behind the Coalition's) held up pretty well.

In the south-east of Australia, New South Wales, the ACT, Victoria and Tasmania, Labor won 42 or 97 seats (44 per cent). In Queensland, Northern Territory, Western Australia and South Australia we won only seven of 51 seats (13 per cent). Loss of infrastructure in outlying states may be the most serious obstacle to winning marginal seats back and regaining government.

The outer states have a history of electoral volatility. In the 1975 election, when there were 127 seats in the House of Representatives, 41 of them in the north and west, in Queensland the ALP won only Oxley, and in Western Australia Fremantle. However, in South Australia, when Don Dunstan was at the height of his popularity, Labor lost only Kingston, holding six of 12 seats.

Andrew Robb, the Liberal campaign director, told the Sydney Institute that in 1996 the Coalition won:

- 47.5 per cent of blue-collar workers (to Labor's 39)

- 47 per cent of the Catholic vote (to Labor's 37)

They could also claim:

- a majority of women
- a majority of Anglos
- a majority of the aged
- a majority of the young.

The Problems

1 **'It's Time'**. After thirteen years in office, this was important psychologically and voters in the exit polls ranked it first (34 per cent). However, it was probably an easy rationalisation ('anyway, they've had a good run') to explain a complex, multi-causal, phenomenon.

2 **Loss of national consensus.** Losing the election was the second worst consequence of 2 March. The worst was the realisation that we deluded ourselves that there was national consensus on issues of race, sexuality, gender and tolerance, and acted accordingly. A more inclusive, more sensitive new vocabulary was attacked as rigid, alienating and ridiculed as being 'politically correct'.

3 **Community anxiety.** We failed to recognise or address a deep-seated mood of community anxiety and grievance. Howard's appeal on the 'Four Corners' program to wanting to make Australians feel 'comfortable and relaxed', seemed ludicrously limited but it actually captured the community's mood very accurately. The Coalition slogan 'For all of us' had a coded meaning picked up by many alienated Labor voters.

4 **Accumulated grievances.** The ALP in government was out of touch with voter sentiment from the late 1980s. It took a long time to catch up with us but in the end the accumulation of grievances was decisive.

5 **Switching off.** There was a perception that we stopped listening— illustrated by a conspicuous failure to understand the significance of the anti-Labor swing in the March 1995

Canberra by-election. Talkback radio identified and encouraged blue-collar alienation.

6 **Hindmarsh Island.** This issue raised concerns about sectional approaches and double standards. (Discrimination for and discrimination against are opposite sides of the same coin.) This case was immensely damaging and used against Labor in the talkback programs.

7 **Isolation of the leadership.** During the campaign, the leadership was sanitised and isolated by excessive campaign 'management' to avoid confrontation with potentially aggrieved voters. There was a serious alienation from journalists (other than John Laws?), contributing to an unwillingness to consider the issues they raised.

8 **Howard's leadership.** We failed to recognise Howard's return to Liberal leadership in January 1995 as a serious challenge. We assumed that Howard was maintaining his 'hard right' position. In fact, he learnt a great deal from 1993. (Did we?)

9 **Misreading the 1993 victory**. We read the 1993 election as a victory for the 'True Believers', rather than as a reaction against Fightback! and the GST. Within a week, Tom Keneally had pointed out that this could be interpreted as exclusive, alienating and self-congratulatory (although understandable).

10 **Recovery encouraged mood for change.** In 1996 the economic recovery may, paradoxically, have acted against us: voters felt they could change without much risk. In 1993, when economic indicators were poor, voters chose between anger against Labor and fear of the GST. Fear won.

11 **Behaviour in Parliament.** Governments invariably bear the blame for political rough-houses, unfair though it is.

12 **Carmen Lawrence–Penny Easton affair.** This paralysed the last session of Parliament, and prevented us from taking the initiative on policy. However, its direct impact in 1996 was limited. (Carmen polled well in Fremantle.)

13 **Affirmative action.** Although our 1994 Conference decisions were not to come into operation until 1 January 1996, we looked (and look) monumentally hypocritical in putting up fewer women in winnable seats in 1996 than we did in 1993, claiming 'special circumstances' in each case.

14 **Privatisation.** Selling off national icons was deeply unpopular and raised questions about what Labor stood for. In the *Financial Review* articles on the Liberal win, Andrew Robb asserted that after the Coalition television advertisements described the Telstra and IBM joint ventures as 'privatisation', focus groups, when asked, 'Which party will sell Telstra?' answered 'Both'.

15 **The republic.** The republic itself was less of an issue than its handling. There was monumental confusion about the roles of head of state and head of government. People thought they would get Keating as president without the opportunity of a direct vote. The UMR polling indicated that the republic was seen as a low priority area and affected few votes.

16 **Multiculturalism.** There was deep uneasiness about some aspects of multiculturalism. Tolerance is one thing, but to many battlers multiculturalism was seen as 'special pleading' or a 'free kick' not available to everybody.

17 **Top-down policy-making.** Which constituency were we responding to on APEC, the Indonesian Treaty, the Information Superhighway, and the Hilmer reforms? None of these issues was ever debated at National Conference. What is the role of branch membership in shaping policy (or even determining preselection)?

18 **Foreign debt.** There was widespread uneasiness about foreign debt and our failure to explain it (especially as it was misunderstood as being 'Commonwealth debt'). Even when the monthly balance of payments figures looked bad, we always explained that they were good news (What would we have said if they actually had *been* good?)

19 **Language problems.** This is a subliminal issue, but it is often raised. We did not communicate in a way that was understood

(especially by Labor's traditional base). The language of economic debate was 'not Labor'. ('a beautiful set of numbers' ... 'This is as good as it gets' ... 'We'll bolt it in ...').

20 **Role of elites and pressure groups.** There were damaging accusations that we cultivated elites and sectional interests and put less emphasis on the mainstream. (It may have been exaggerated, but the perception was strong.)

21 **The 'S' word.** We had an incapacity to say: 'We were wrong. We are sorry ...' and this contributed to a sense that we were arrogant. (Channel 9's 'worm' gave the biggest response to John Howard in the first debate with Paul Keating when he said: 'I was wrong on Medicare ...'.)

22 **Priorities–balance.** There was a community misconception about priorities–balance in government, as if we could either have the republic OR drought relief, the republic OR reduced foreign debt, the republic OR lower youth unemployment, but not both. It was a classic example of a false antithesis. There was a failure to explain how governments, typically, were handling scores of issues simultaneously.

23 **Declining role for Caucus.** Little opportunity for frank debate. With few exceptions, we lacked courage. Every criticism or expression of concern was treated as a matter of confidence.

24 **Blue-collar workers.** These workers resented our cultivation of the big end of town.

25 **The 1993 budget.** It was seen as a breach of faith, especially the (unavoidable) withdrawal of the L.A.W. tax cuts. (George Bush suffered in the same way in 1992 over 'Read my lips: no new taxes'.)

26 **Woodchips, jobs and environment.** The logging dispute and the blockage of Parliament exposed seemingly intractable conflicts between two of Labor's important constituencies: unionised blue-collar workers and environmentalists.

27 **Targeted welfare.** This aroused real antagonism from many traditional supporters who felt that some groups (e.g. single

mothers, Aborigines), for whatever reason, were receiving special treatment.

28 **The Accord.** This was seen as a great success in our early years but turned sour when many unionists felt their living standards were eroding, and they were not consoled by the social safety net and tax reductions.

29 **Change fatigue.** Award restructuring, enterprise agreements, the move away from collective bargaining, all contributed to a weariness about change, and we were the losers.

30 **Eroding the role of government.** Labor's newfound commitment to economic rationalisation and privatisation undercut the legitimacy or moral base of government. Privatisation was underpinned by the assumption that governments always handled things badly. If we downgrade the capacity or role of government, it is hardly surprising if voters make harsh judgments about parties in power.

There were some negatives during the last weeks of the campaign:

31 **The 'Asians won't talk to Howard' claim.** Should voters decide with Mahathir or Soeharto in mind?

32 **'No show' on budget figures.** This gave the impression that there was something to hide.

33 **Bill Kelty.** His remarks had the potential for misconstruction and we failed to explain them. (Nor did he!)

34 **The 'letter affair'.** This stopped any political movement back in the last days of campaigning when many voters were still undecided.

The Ten Commandments:

The ALP stands for:

1 Redefining and asserting Australia's national interest. This would include economic, social and Constitutional elements, maintaining control of national institutions, and the right of

government to maintain core responsibilities, including ownership where appropriate, in areas with social impact (e.g. communications, utilities, law and order, health, education).

2 Improving wages and working conditions internationally, including the ending of child labour and promoting fair trading, while remaining in the global economy.

3 Using taxation as a social instrument, to be progressive and based on wealth.

4 Insisting that community values are more important than market forces, including a commitment to power sharing and affirmative action.

5 Ensuring access, equity and security in education, health, civil and legal rights, the arts and leisure, and information.

6 Promoting national unity while recognising the value of ethnic and cultural diversity.

7 Guaranteeing the protection of soil, air and water, and promoting global environmental cooperation (e.g. on global warming).

8 Working out policies in an integrated rather than segmented fashion, so that, for example, employment and the environment are considered together, not in isolation.

9 Reconciling mainstream Australia with Aborigines and Torres Strait Islanders.

10 Providing access to full and appropriate employment for those able and willing to work, maintaining support for the principle of collective bargaining, the Industrial Relations Commission and the Australian Council of Trade Unions.

Chapter 2

Principles, Policies and Politics; Getting Labor Back on Track

Gary Gray

There are a series of issues that need to be canvassed after Labor's electoral defeat. They centre on the crucial interplay of principles, policy and politics. They are about getting the Australian Labor Party back on track. About returning Labor to government.

My focus is on how we can fashion our political agenda and take the initiative from the conservatives.

All that we do, *must* be biased towards action, not towards analysis for its own sake.

Our ideas must be intellectually, economically and socially coherent.

A lot of what we have to do is essential and strategic. A lot of it is pretty basic, not inspirational or earth-shattering, but laborious, patient, painstaking, nuts-and-bolts political hard slog. It is what many thought was beneath them in the last part of our period in government — the things we did not do which lost us government by default.

We need to look hard and honestly at how we lost, because understanding how not to lose — how not to repeat our mistakes — is necessary for getting Labor back on track.

But this is not the whole solution. We must also return to good policies based on Labor principle — that is good politics. Our plan for the future must be a combination of principle, policies and politics that join with our experience of governing.

But even the most pragmatic, action-oriented plan has to take account of the trends and changes we can see gathering force around us.

We need to look at those trends and directions, and try to align ourselves with them.

We cannot be a relevant and effective mainstream political force if we are simply against things, any more than Canute could make the tide recede to suit his timetable for the invasion of Britain.

We must make the effort and take the risk of thinking ahead — at the same time as we bear in mind the realities and practicalities of effective political action.

The Australian Labor Party has always produced both pragmatists and visionaries. That is a huge political strength.

At the same time we have a history of pitching our visionaries against our pragmatists. And that is a central weakness.

We need both. Above all, we need to have both visionaries and pragmatists working together in a coherent continuum of politics and policies. That's the way forward, to a future for the party and for Australia that is; fair and realistic. idealistic and practical. ethical and effective.

Change

Change is the only certainty for the future. And there are three kinds of change I think we need to factor in to our planning for the years ahead.

The first is social and economic change which is occurring at a level at least partly outside the Australian context, and over which we have limited influence.

The second is change related to the actions of the current government.

And the third broad area of change we have to face is internal. What can we do, as a party, to make ourselves better fit to govern?

These three tiers of change are worth differentiating, because they remind us that there are limits to what government, any government, can achieve. We also need to recognise that the major issues we face are a combination of all three types and tiers of change, in differing proportions.

Take the globalisation of Australia's economy as an example. Globalisation is not a local Australian phenomenon, but it is impacting on every aspect of our productive capability, and on the whole structure of employment.

No government can opt out. But government has a key role in determining the way global forces impact on Australia and Australian families.

Labor's response was to distribute the economic benefits of participation in the global economy in a way which provided a safety net, an effective insurance system for the displaced, and which delivered equality of opportunity.

The conservative way is to allow the market to determine success or failure, and to blame the displaced for their own uncompetitiveness. Labor uses the public sector as a balancing mechanism in the struggle between individual pain and community benefit. The conservative agenda is to dismantle the public sector, in order to free up the individual to pursue self-interest alone.

Our task for the future will be to rebuild, redefine and renew our social infrastructure. The old ALP — the ALP of the 1950s and 1960s, the wilderness years — would have said just 'turn back the clock' — reject 'the inevitable' — and by passing a resolution at an ALP Conference they would have felt … good.

We cannot do that. We have to deal with realities. It was the Hawke government which had the courage to expose Australia to the global economy. Australia had to accept the challenge of global trade; we knew then, and we know now that the benefits outweigh the pain of structural adjustment.

We had to accept the fact that Australia is a low tax country, that we will never have Scandinavian levels of taxation and that the task of government was to distribute revenues effectively and fairly — to achieve equality of opportunity. The days of universal benefits were and are over, they would not and will not return.

In these two examples we dealt with just two realities; two inevitable forces — world trade and scarce tax resources. These realities made our political packaging harder, but not impossible. For the future it means we have to be able to explain and manage the inevitable consequences of, for instance, global trade (the pressure on our manufacturing sector, and the shrinking number of jobs available in it), and the avoidable consequences (a disenfranchised underclass).

Getting that crucial difference across will be a major political challenge for us. We did it in the 1980s while we controlled the agenda. Then we let it slip; we gave our agenda away.

It hurts to acknowledge that we gave the agenda away — but that is how the electorate saw it.

They thought Medicare, education, workplace security and superannuation would be all right under Howard.

That lies at the heart of why we lost in March 1996. We allowed our opponents to suggest to the people that they would have done what we did; the perception became reality and they stole our agenda — or so Australians thought.

The only comfort we have is that they will not be able to pull off the same sleight of hand again. The evidence against their ability to manage the forces of change is already mounting up.

Getting back to government

Labor lost office in 1996 for four reasons.

First we became complacent. We believed we had a magic formula — even a genius for winning the unwinnable — like we had in 1993.

Then we got distracted; we lost the mainstream. We traded the support of our own people for the cheers of the loudest 'interest groups'. Occasionally this made us into social engineers … telling people what was acceptable.

Then we became bureaucrats. As a result, we missed the mood, and failed to notice the ranks thinning out behind us.

And finally, we entered the campaign on the back foot and stayed there. People thought our opponents had stolen our clothes.

Fundamentally, we are responsible for the Coalition victory of 2 March. We let them win by default, not during the campaign but in government. And the sooner and more thoroughly we digest that unappetising fact, the less likely we are ever to take political success for granted again.

If we are brutal about our analysis, we are faced with two

choices: either the electorate let us down, or we let them down. And the people are very clear about their perception of where the fault lay: they told us in no uncertain terms that 'the Party changed, not us'.

In their perceptions, we drifted away from the values which we have always endorsed. Our commitment to a fair day's work for a fair day's wage, equality of opportunity, and collective responsibility.

Against this perception, we did understand and act upon basic Labor principles by striking the right balance, for instance, between collective responsibility and individual rights.

In government, we pursued both sides of that balance with vigour and commitment. When we had to cut spending, as we did in the late 1980s, we were consistently fair — we built a model of fairness out of our targeted benefits system. Labor's model is the envy of social democratic parties around the world. We committed ourselves to providing a safety net — a national form of insurance — which helped those who were hurt by the massive changes which were called 'structural adjustment' or 'micro economic reform'.

At the same time our policies were designed to allow individuals the greatest possible opportunity to succeed. That is our commitment to individual rights. And together they make for good Labor government.

We introduced universal superannuation. We created sustainable jobs. We pinned our colours to the goal of fairness. That is collective responsibility.

Individual rights and collective responsibility make for commonsense government.

Medicare is a great example of the collective responsibility to pay for and maintain a cost-effective health system and the individual right to quality health care. The health of one person or one family is a collective concern and responsibility.

By contrast the Liberals, the conservatives, philosophically, subordinate collective responsibility to individual rights. And already we are starting to see just how different this policy direction is.

So you see in thirteen years of office federally we do have a lot to be proud of.

We can say — with justifiable pride — that, at our best, we did well.

But I am not making these declarations to make us all feel better. Just the opposite, in fact. My purpose is to point out just what we have put at risk by our failure to control the agenda.

If the conservatives believed as we do in the principles of fairness and equality of opportunity, then losing government would not matter so much. Our legacy — and the foundations on which it was built — would survive a change of management. We could regroup and come back to pick up where we left off.

But that is not the case. Our opponents are not the same as us. Ideology is not dead; it just played dead. It was a sleeping dog, and we let it lie.

For that reason, our loss of government was not in any sense trivial; it was, ultimately, a failure to protect our own. It was also a betrayal of good politics. And our people will pay the price of that betrayal in direct proportion to the length of time we remain in Opposition.

So our absolute focus must be on regaining government — not for the sake of office, but for the people who need us to protect them from what can be, and might well be, an insecure future.

The point is that we live in a world where most people, with quite good reason, feel powerless and threatened. It is a world where they search for security and certainty.

What we value, as Labor people, needs to be stated and restated, not taken for granted or left to grow mouldy from disuse. We need to engage people in the political process, and galvanise them into action to defend what we otherwise might lose.

For at our core we are the party of security, of certainty.

We are the party of principle.

We have an obligation to get our principles, our policies and our politics rights.

Now we have an opportunity to rebuild. We have lost some good people. We have to find others. More talented. More promising and more committed, to replace them. We need to capture the people with passion, the people who share our principles, and give them good reason to participate.

We need to continue to rebuild Labor's resources, and to use those resources effectively and creatively. We must regenerate our traditional ascendancy in the realm of ideas, and take back our leadership of the intellectual agenda.

We need policies which are targeted and relevant. We need ideas on how to ride the waves of change that lie ahead, and ideas which restore the community's belief in Labor as the party — the only party — that knows how to deliver maximum economic benefit while protecting the families who pay the social cost.

We need to recommit to the fundamental values and principles we all share.

And we need to do so publicly and explicitly.

That means attacking our opponents where it hurts. The Coalition have never liked spelling out their ideology; they prefer to express it indirectly, through marginalising the weak.

That explains their attitude to welfare fraud. Commonsense says that welfare fraud cannot be tolerated. But is the Dole Diary the right solution?

It also explains the savagery of the Coalition cuts to jobs programs — like Skillshare. Commonsense says you do not create more jobs by cutting back on programs.

The reason they do not like to expose their beliefs to the light of day is that their ideas are threadbare. Naked self-interest does not (yet) constitute a philosophy that Australians are proud to espouse.

And that is where Labor holds the high ground. We are and should be proud of our achievements. Because they reflect beliefs and principles with which we are happy to identify.

But the fact that those beliefs and principles are right will not guarantee their survival or their victory. We have to practise them, and show that they work — that they deliver the practical, tangible benefits of security, mutual consideration and, ultimately, compassion.

The connection between Labor principles and our policies was not lost during our thirteen years of government, but we came to take it for granted and we let it fall below the horizon of consciousness — both inside the party and outside in the electorate. We failed politically.

On my reading of the situation, that was a massive error, and a betrayal of ourselves, our beliefs and our people. It must not be repeated.

But there is a silver lining — or at least a thread of comfort. The Australian electorate did not vote against Labor's beliefs and principles in March 1996; they just forgot, like we did, that Labor's values are not universal, not part of the natural order of things, and not to be taken for granted.

They have to be fought for, and defended not just in an election campaign but all the time.

Finally when your basic principles — fairness, collective responsibility and opportunity — are right, you must strive to get the policies which implement these principles right too. Good policies lead to good politics. And it is effective political communication that will win arguments about policy objectives.

Winning the argument wins votes.

Getting Labor on track is about principles, policies and politics.

Chapter 3

The Challenge of Economic Policy: Putting People First

Gareth Evans

Labor's core values

The traditional Labor Party approach to economic policy has been built around a number of core values. We believe in meeting the needs of ordinary working people; we believe in helping those who are socially and economically disadvantaged; and we believe in the role of government not only in achieving these objectives but in securing many public goods — like first-class education and medical research, the enjoyment of culture and the protection of our environmental heritage — which are simply unlikely to be delivered as effectively, if at all, by the private sector and the free market.

Economic policy always involves choice. There are many ways of measuring a country's economic health — among them growth, employment, inflation, interest rates, budget balances, public debt, foreign debt and current account balances. Circumstances are never so ideal that every single one of those indicators is simultaneously at its best possible setting. And particular policy responses tend to have impacts that push against each other. What may be helpful in reducing a budget deficit may not be at all helpful in reducing unemployment or in building competitive productive capacity in the longer term; conversely, what may immediately stimulate growth or reduce unemployment might generate longer term structural problems.

It has to be acknowledged that sometimes economic necessity will demand all-out priority attention being given to a particular problem — like exploding inflation or a manifestly unmanageable current account deficit. In these circumstances, particular restrictionist policy strategies will for all practical purposes be compelled, whoever is in power. But more often than not governments do have the capacity to choose between competing policy approaches, and as often as not standard economic logic will simply expose the options — rather than compel a particular choice. In these more familiar circumstances it is, at the end of the day, philosophical preference, whether acknowledged or not, that will determine the policy choice.

The traditional Labor philosophy has been, very simply, that the first priority for economic policy should always be *people*. The basic objective is to improve people's living standards — through providing sustainable full employment and rising incomes. Everything else — controlling inflation, reducing current account deficits, bringing budgets into surplus, reducing public debt, reducing foreign debt and improving savings — are second and third order objectives by comparison. They are means to the achievement of the primary objective of improving people's living standards, not ends in themselves.

I believe that these principles, and this general approach, continue to command assent throughout the labor movement, and also would be seen by the majority of the wider community as relevant and attractive. But how successfully have we translated those principles into practice in the past? Do we have anything to answer for in the conduct of our economic policy over the years in which we held the reins? And what does all this mean for us in confronting the economic environment of Australia in the late 1990s — not least on the battleground of the 1996 Budget, where a number of fundamental choices have now been very starkly exposed indeed?

Labor in government

By no means did we manage to get everything right in our thirteen years of government — no government ever does — and we certainly did not explain ourselves, especially to our traditional supporters, as clearly and directly as we might have. But I believe our record of economic management, through a very difficult period of internationally driven change, stands up very well indeed against the principles just outlined. The key elements in that record are:

- We dragged the economy back from the disaster we inherited from the Fraser–Howard government — a budget deficit equivalent to $24 billion in today's dollars, with unemployment at 10 per cent and inflation simultaneously at 11.4 per cent.

- We confronted the reality, becoming ever clearer through the 1970s but ignored by our predecessors, that the luck of the lucky country, able to depend first on agriculture and then on mineral and energy resources, was beginning to well and truly run out — and that we had to make ourselves export-competitive in manufacturing and services if we were to maintain, let alone improve, the living standards of ordinary Australians. Not least through persistent jawboning, we developed a new export culture in the country, and one specifically focused on our place in the Asia Pacific region.

- We put in place, albeit often with a good deal of transitional pain, the raft of policies necessary to make us export competitive. We floated the dollar, and brought competition and lower prices to banking, air travel and telecommunications. We broke down tariff walls, and brought greater efficiency to shipping and the waterfront. Our industrial relations policies produced major economic gains and unprecedented industrial peace.

- We changed the shape of the economy as a result. We left an economy around 40 per cent more competitive than it had been a decade earlier. Our firms capitalised on our increased competitiveness, and our exports grew faster than those of the rest of the world. We grasped the opportunities of our region, and led the way in establishing new forums like APEC to bring trade and jobs to Australian firms and workers.

Australia today is less reliant on commodities, and less vulnerable to world cycles; we export more manufactured goods, especially high value added goods; and we are moving faster than the rest of the world into the boom growth area of service exports.

- We grew the economy over the whole period at an average rate of 3.7 per cent, and employment at an average of 2.2 per cent, generating over 2 million new jobs in the process.

- We overhauled the nation's education and training systems to gear them to the challenges of competing in the international economy. We dramatically improved school retention rates: by 1993, 78 per cent of our 19-year-olds were completing either Year 12 or a post-schooling qualification: this compared with the less than 30 per cent rate John Howard left in 1983. We introduced Working Nation to offer those with the least skills, especially the long-term unemployed, the training and work experience they need to compete effectively in the labour market: one of the most important initiatives to enhance our nation's human capital ever seen in this country.

- We removed inflation as a problem in the Australian economy. At double-digit levels in 1983, since the early 1990s inflation has averaged just 2 per cent a year.

- We addressed the savings problem endemic in Australia, by producing in the late 1980s four budget surpluses, unique in Australia's post-war history, and by implementing a revolutionary superannuation strategy to build up private saving. Superannuation, once the preserve of the wealthy and public sector workers, is now provided to 90 per cent of all employees.

- We markedly decreased the tax burden for all workers, with seven rounds of tax cuts for personal income over our time in office. The bottom marginal tax rate was lowered by us from 30 per cent under Howard as treasurer to 20 per cent, with the tax-free threshold raised. Australia is now (after Turkey) the second lowest taxed country in the OECD.

- We achieved both economic and social justice objectives through our eight successive Accords in partnership with the trade union movement, delivering wage restraint and productivity gains that have been crucial in underpinning low inflation and steady employment growth. That faith has been rewarded with tax relief and substantial improvements in the social wage: including through Medicare, child-care benefits, family payments, rent assistance and low income rebates. While real average earnings increased modestly by 6.9 per cent over our period in office, real household disposable income per capita rose by 21 per cent.

- We ensured, through many additional assistance measures, that necessary wage restraint did not impact unfairly on lowest income families: with family payments up to $121 a fortnight for each child, parenting allowances of up to $280 a fortnight for low-income families as well as $500 million annually in rent assistance and access to a Health Care Card, with all associated benefits.

The scale of our achievement can be very simply summarised.

We inherited from John Howard in 1983 an economy that was on the rocks and breaking up — inward looking and uncompetitive, with high unemployment, high inflation, high interest rates, massive industrial conflict, and obvious massive social inequities — including 2 million people without guaranteed access to health care.

We bequeathed back to John Howard in 1996 a structurally sound and internationally competitive economy, which he himself was obliged to concede last month was 'better than just good in parts' — one with high growth, low inflation, falling unemployment, greatly enhanced social equity, and with its fundamental forces better balanced than they have been at any time in the last twenty-five years.

The economy

There are still some problems with the Australian economy, but none of them are unmanageable or cause for alarm. They can and should be sensibly addressed by thoughtful, balanced and moderate strategies — strategies which, in accordance with Labor's philosophy, put people first.

The first and most serious continuing problem, and the one which impacts most directly upon people, is unemployment. Like every other industrialised economy, we have been hit over the last decade by a combination of dramatic changes — in particular the cost competition pressures of globalisation, the large-scale entry of women into the workforce and the explosive expansion of computer technology. These have together conspired to make realistic and acceptable medium-term unemployment targets like our 5 per cent by the year 2000 — a target which not so many years ago would have been quite unacceptably high.

We now have 760 000 unemployed people, 8.3 per cent of the labour force. This is an unhappy figure, but it should be kept in context. The participation rate — the proportion of those of working age seeking work — has risen very significantly since 1983, largely as a result of the welcome and overdue entrance of women into the workforce: if the participation rate were the same now as it was in 1983, the present unemployment rate would now be no more than 4 per cent. And had job creation remained throughout our term at the same low level it was under John Howard as treasurer, unemployment would be over 2 million now, with an unemployment rate of 23 per cent!

The way to address our continuing unemployment problem is not to go down the deregulatory American path on which the Howard government is now embarked with its industrial relations legislation. Kim Beazley put it eloquently in a recent speech to the AMWU: 'People are not commodities ... Labour is not just another commodity'. It is simply not acceptable in our society, and with our tradition of equity and fairness, he said, 'to "clear" labour markets in the same way you clear the copper market, by dropping the price until suppliers leave or demand picks up'.

The way to cut back unemployment is rather by economic strategies designed to keep growth running at a sustainable 4 per cent or better. When we averaged 4 per cent growth over our last three years in government, we not only beat our 1993 target of

500 000 new jobs, which the Coalition had scoffed at, but exceeded it by over 40 per cent, creating well over 700 000 jobs (70 per cent of them in small business since 1993), putting us well on the way to achieving our stated target of 5 per cent unemployment by the year 2000. All this has obvious implications for budgetary policy, to which I will return shortly.

The second significant problem still evident in the Australian economy is the current account deficit. Although likely to come in for 1995–96 at some $7 billion less than the previous financial year, falling as a percentage of GDP from around 6 per cent the previous year to 4 per cent, a current account deficit of this order of magnitude is a constraint on growth, and we would be much more comfortable with it running at no more than 2–3 per cent of GDP.

That said, the problem is perfectly manageable at the moment, and one that should sensibly be addressed as a medium-term priority, not one demanding all-stops-out immediate action. The difficulty is not with merchandise trade, which continues to be more or less in balance, or even with services, but rather with net income, in particular interest payments to service debt borrowed abroad. But Australia's net foreign debt is not especially dramatic by international standards: at 38.8 per cent it is less than in a number of other OECD countries — including New Zealand (with only 8 per cent of it owed by the Commonwealth government, 60 per cent being private). Moreover, the debt service ratio — the proportion of our exports needed to pay interest on outstanding debt — is presently a comfortable 11.6 per cent (way down on the peak of 20.6 per cent in 1990).

Certainly it is nonsensical to argue — as Peter Costello continues to do — that a major budget deficit reduction exercise will translate directly into an improved current account. While it is perfectly true that the key to longer term improvement in the current account is greater national saving (assuming that no-one wants to reduce domestic investment), a reduction in government dissaving by reducing the budget deficit will not translate directly into a reduction in the current account deficit unless private savings and investment behaviour remain absolutely constant — and in the real world (as proponents of simplistic 'twin deficit' theories now have to concede), that simply does not happen. The huge effort made by Labor to generate budget surpluses in the late 1980s did not make any direct impact on our current account deficit then, and there is no reason to assume a similar exercise would have any different impact now.

The message is that government dissaving does have to be addressed, and it is desirable for this reason for budgets to be in balance or better, but this objective should not be pursued in a way that cuts across other goals, inhibiting the solution of more pressing problems. Putting people first means not ignoring the current account problem, but — in the present environment — treating it as a lower priority one than hauling back unemployment.

The third and remaining problem or, in this instance, alleged problem, with the Australian economy at the moment is the size of the Commonwealth budget deficit after nearly five years of continuous economic growth. The precise size, and certainly the significance, of that deficit is a matter of intense political controversy.

Whether the starting underlying deficit for 1996–97 is $8.9 billion, as Costello is currently claiming, or anything like that figure, continues to depend on official estimates about future growth and inflation rates. Those estimates have been wrong in the past (not least for the 1995–96 financial year just completed, when inflation proved significantly lower than predicted, and revenue fell accordingly). And with the best will and the most competence in the world, such estimates are bound to be wrong, to a greater or lesser extent, in the future. But what does seem clear is that the growth estimates for 1996–97 will be revised up on budget night from their present 3 per cent to at least 3.75 per cent. And with that revision — and some accompanying likely downward revision in the GDP deflator measure of inflation — a significant proportion of the alleged problem will disappear.

Even if the starting underlying budget deficit for 1996–97 were to prove to be of its present alleged order of magnitude, there are some very important points to make about its significance.

The first is that a deficit of around 1.5 per cent of GDP is not massive, or even very large by international standards: certainly it was not regarded as alarming by any of the key economic policy-makers and financial institution players I spoke to in the course of visits I have made recently to the financial capitals of East Asia and North America. The OECD estimates our deficit to be, with that of the United States, the third lowest, after Denmark and Norway, of the major industrialised countries. Some of these comparisons cannot be made too often. Not only is our tax–GDP ratio the second lowest in the OECD, as already stated, but our public sector expenditure is the third lowest (after the USA and Japan), and our net government debt is the fourth lowest (after Japan, Norway and Finland).

The second point to make is that the make-up or character of any country's budget deficit is as significant as its size. The key to understanding why the present Australian deficit is still apparently quite large, notwithstanding several years of positive growth, is simply our success in tackling inflation — with all the benefits that has brought for competitiveness, investment, saving and social equity. The low inflation rates we have now achieved have made the task of restoring the budget to surplus in the 1990s much more difficult than used to be the case. In the past governments could simply rely on the magic of fiscal drag to automatically generate a rapid and expanding pool of revenue without having to make any budgetary changes, but that luxury is no longer available.

Other factors that have contributed significantly to present budgetary balance problems have been Labor's progressive tariff reforms, which have denied us increasing amounts of revenue each year, some $6 billion worth in 1996–97; Labor's decision in government to shield the states from the largest impact of the fiscal fallout of the recession by maintaining general purpose payments in real terms while Commonwealth revenue collapsed; and in particular Labor's decision to make a massive expenditure commitment to education, training and job readiness programs, building a skilled human capital base for the future.

What is absolutely clear is that the significant deterioration in the underlying budget outcome for 1995–96 as compared with that predicted in May 1995, which in turn has set back the base on which this year's budget has to be constructed, was not in any way the product of an unjustified blow-out in spending.

Nearly all of the change — over 87 per cent of it — was due to changed parameters: in other words Treasury and Finance had their forecasts, of inflation especially, quite wrong. The forward estimates for this year are simply not riddled with wasteful spending commitments: that is why it is simply not possible to find $8 billion worth of cuts without hacking into valuable, efficient and well-targeted programs.

The third point, and in many ways most important point of all, to make about the budget deficit is that, on Costello's own figures, the problem that he and his government have claimed to be so exercised about is one that is largely self-correcting over the life of this Parliament. In March the treasurer estimated — with very conservative 3 per cent growth assumptions — that, without any policy changes, the purported $8 billion black hole would be reduced to just over $3 billion by 1998–99. Even factoring in, as he now has, the $1.3 billion slippage from last financial year, it is completely possible to get to underlying balance within three years with just a fraction of the budget cuts now being proposed by the government.

This is because on entirely reasonable assumptions — for example those recently published by Banker's Trust economists, involving real economic growth higher and CPI inflation lower than in the latest published Treasury estimates — for the 1998–99 financial year the underlying Budget deficit would be no more than around $2 billion. And a $2 billion savings task is obviously whole orders of magnitude easier to achieve than the $8 billion task the government is still claiming to be necessary.

The Howard government

Against the background I have been sketching it is not hard to expose both the economic wrong-headedness and the crudely political nature of the government's present behaviour.

First, the wrong-headed economics. The last thing the Australian economy needs just now is a sharp and savage dose of contraction. While inflation is manifestly under control, growth at the 4 per cent level needed to bite into unemployment is simply not assured. After a year in which employment has grown by only 1 per cent, and unemployment has stuck at around 8 per cent, there is a pressing need to generate new employment growth.

Private sector economists, including Westpac and Access Economics, estimate that $4 billion cuts in each of the next two years will mean less GDP growth each year than would otherwise have occurred. In other words, instead of working to help the economy maintain 4 per cent-or-better growth, the cuts will work in exactly the opposite way. Apart from the tens of thousands of jobs now being directly cut out of the Public Service, cutting away growth on this scale means throwing away the opportunity to create some 80 000 new jobs over the next two years.

It cannot be assumed that the cuts will translate into a massive rise in business confidence, with new investment 'crowding in' as a compensating consequence. Recent surveys have shown business investment expectations to be in fact already quite buoyant — with planned increases of around 20 per cent in 1997 — so there is simply not the scope for an additional increase in private investment of the magnitude that would be necessary to offset the blow of the proposed cuts on the economy.

It is now being argued by Costello that a deficit reduction exercise on the scale the government is proposing would be quickly rewarded by interest rate cuts — and that this is another reason why the government should be applauded for its application to the task. But while a savagely contractionary budget will of course create its own momentum for interest rate cuts, they will come not as a reward for good fiscal behaviour but rather as either a reward for our excellent recent inflation record or as a necessary corrective for an economy with the stuffing knocked out of it.

One of the worst economic consequences of the proposed cuts is their impact on education, training and other labour market programs which have been designed specifically not just to help individuals lead more rewarding lives but to strengthen the capacity of the whole economy to perform competitively in the future. The American President's Council of Economic Advisers Chairman, Dr Joseph Stiglitz, sounded this warning in unequivocal terms at the recent OECD ministerial meeting:

We must also recognize that deficit reduction is not an end in itself, but a means for increasing living standards and growth by raising available savings and fostering investment. This has one strong implication: How we cut matters. Too often, governments under fiscal stress cut spending on research and development, training, and other investments — gutting the very policies that have the greatest effect on long term economic growth and opportunity.

But this is a warning that has gone unheeded by the Howard government.

There is certainly a case, given Australia's weak savings performance and the state of our current account deficit, for reducing government dissaving. Targeting for budget balance or better is a legitimate and proper objective — one that we would certainly have continued to pursue had we stayed in office. But to choose to achieve that target through savage budget cuts within an excessively abbreviated time frame is simply economically wrong-headed, given the manageability of the current account problem in the short to medium term and, by contrast, the seriousness and urgency of our unemployment problem.

It is the choice of a government that certainly does *not* put people first — that is bent rather on the pursuit of a radical Thatcherite small-government ideology; which sees virtue in cutting the size of public sector personnel and programs as an end in itself; and which is either blind or indifferent to the pain it will cause ordinary working people and the harm it will cause the economy.

Our choice, by contrast, would be to target a return to budgetary balance by 1998–99, setting ourselves in the process a savings task, to be achieved by that time, of some $2 billion. We have already pointed out, before the election (in Treasurer Willis's detailed statement of 28 February) a number of measures which would make significant inroads on that target, and it pales into relative insignificance by comparison with the over $30 billion worth (in 1995 dollars) of reduction in outlays we progressively achieved over our thirteen years in government.

Now, as to the politics...

The Coalition's behaviour from the outset has been governed far more by political opportunism than any genuine sense of economic necessity, but the honeymoon mist has tended to conceal until now just how crude that behaviour has been. There are four distinct charges in the indictment.

The first charge is that the Coalition's 'discovery' of the so-called $8 billion 'Beazley black hole' was deliberately contrived to place the blame on Labor for the pain associated with the general expenditure cutting and program slashing it was determined to embark upon anyway for its own Thatcherite small-government ideological reasons.

Whatever the accuracy of the growth and inflation projections on which they were based, the truth is that before last Christmas 1995 predictions were being made by Treasury officials and many in the private sector of a significant deficit outcome for 1995–96 which would flow through into 1996–97. As Max Walsh put it in the *Sydney Morning Herald* on 10 May 1996:

> If there was the slightest surprise by John Howard or Peter Costello when they were told that the prospective deficit for 1996–97 was $8 billion then you would be concerned about their competence. That figure was in everybody's ballpark. That is why the demonising of Kim Beazley and his black hole has, for me at least, a lack of credibility.

The second charge is that the 'Beazley black hole' was really just a further Costello con designed to divert attention from the Coalition's own $4 billion credibility problem in the costing of its pre-election promises (to spend $6.8 billion over the next three years) — promises even more irresponsible had the Coalition *genuinely* believed that it would be confronted with a big deficit legacy from the Labor government.

There is no doubt that the Coalition's promises were ludicrously underfunded. Before the election the Finance Department specifically found $1.2 billion worth of error in the Coalition's *Meeting Our Commitments* calculations — in the form of unachievable savings or underestimated expenditure; another $1.3 billion involved costs that were unavoidable if Coalition policies were implemented; and there was a further $1.4 billion funding shortfall arising from the $3.3 billion of proposed measures which were too vague for even Finance to cost. No information that has emerged since the election has done anything but reinforce that shortfall analysis.

The Coalition's 'family tax package' election bribe, which we will no doubt see triumphantly reannounced in the 1996 budget, is manifestly inequitable in its application (providing, for example, exactly the same benefits to a family earning $70 000 as a family earning $20 000). But it can also only be paid for by a frenzy of cost-cutting programs which will, among other things, decimate labour market programs, vandalise higher education, emasculate our export drive, damage our relations with our Asian neighbours and take away resources from the most vulnerable and needy members of our own community. The Howard government has taken political bribery to new levels of effrontery — not only offering bribes which it says with another face that the economy cannot afford, but stealing the bribe money as well!

The third charge is that the Howard–Costello government is taking political promise-breaking to breathtaking new levels of brazenness. To take just those budgetary promise breaches about which there can at this stage be absolutely no doubt, without speculating about what is yet to be announced, we have:

- the introduction of new taxes on imports — against the pledge that 'there will be no new taxes and no increases in existing taxation under a Coalition government'

- the cuts to higher education — with only the size still to be declared — against the promise 'to maintain the level the funding of operating grants to universities'

- the cuts to Skillshare, NEIS, LEAP, Jobskills and the New Work Opportunities programs and to CES offices — with again only the size to be finalised — against the promise to 'maintain the expenditure on labour market programs in real terms'

- the cut of $65 million to the ABC — against the promise to 'maintain existing funding for the ABC'

- the ending of the R&D tax concession on syndication — against pledges to 'maintain support for R&D through the 150 per cent tax concession' and previous expressions of concern about changes to the syndication scheme 'drying up' effective mobilisation of venture capital

- the announced abolition of regional funding — against the pledge to 'maintain funding for regional development at $150 million over four years'

- the cuts to State Financial Assistance Grants and Special Purpose Payments — against the pledge to provide a 'fixed share of Commonwealth revenue' which would be 'revenue neutral'.

It is difficult to believe that against this background anyone could ever again take at face value any promise made by any member of the Howard–Costello government.

The fourth charge, and this is just about the biggest scam of all, although so far the least remarked, is that what this government is about with its $8 billion worth of budget cutting is not fiscal rectitude and economic responsibility but a crudely political exercise to put itself in a position to buy the next general election due by March 1999.

As we have seen, there will be in 1998–99 — on the government's own figures, supplemented by some reasonably cautious further assumptions about growth and inflation — an underlying budget deficit not much more than $2 billion. That means that if there are $8 billion worth of cuts over the next two years, the budget by 1998–99 will not merely in balance but in surplus to the tune of some $6 billion. Even if the deficit reduction outcome is $7 billion or less (as has been suggested in the last few days, as the acceptable slash-options narrow even for these Huns and Visigoths) the surplus would be of the order of $5 billion.

As we saw as early as 1977 with the 'fistful of dollars' campaign, and as recently as the 1996 election with the nearly

$7 billion worth of family tax and related promises, John Howard has a long track record of bribing his way to government. With a war-chest of $5 billion or $6 billion available, it is not difficult to see how this scenario will play out again in 1999.

The only complication for John Howard is that if the government proceeds to the double dissolution in mid-1997 for which it is now blatantly positioning itself, this will be in the middle of the pain part of the cycle it is now creating — and too early for the government to reach into its forthcoming war-chest. This consideration is no doubt why we are now beginning to see reports that the government is in fact planning to defer its double dissolution until the last constitutionally possible moment in 1998, just six months before the next election is due!

All this political manoeuvring and promise-breaking might be marginally excusable if there were a genuinely powerful economic rationale for achieving budgetary balance — or surplus — within the abbreviated time frame proposed. But, as I have argued throughout this essay, given the real nature and relative scale of Australia's remaining economic problems at this time, the compelling economic logic points in a very different direction — namely to a budget balance by 1998–99 which could much less painfully be achieved.

All this means that Labor in Opposition will be much less tolerant of the government's deficit reduction proposals, and much more willing to expose each of them individually to scrutiny and, where appropriate, attack, than would have been the case if we thought that the government was genuinely and honestly confronting a real economic crisis. In addressing CEDA in April I spelt out some of the key criteria that would determine our reaction to government economic initiatives, including:

- whether they put at risk sustainable economic growth and the living standards of ordinary Australians

- whether they involve broken election promises

- whether they offend values for which we in the labor movement have traditionally stood — in particular equity, distributive justice, the protection of those in need, and the provision of public goods which are incapable of being delivered as well, or at all, by the private sector alone.

Of course it is the case that elected governments must be allowed to govern, and bear the consequences of any misgovernment at the ballot box, in accordance with proper constitutional processes. But while we are not going to revisit 1975, the government should be drafting its budget in the full knowledge that, for all the reasons I have spelt out in this essay, we regard a significant number of its likely components as simply indefensible.

Tactics

I have been dealing in this essay primarily with the familiar set of great macro-economic policy issues which are the staple of mainstream press and parliamentary debate and to which, whether in government or opposition, we have continually to respond. My central argument has been that it is critical for our unity and credibility as a labour movement, and alternative government, that we respond to those issues along the lines of our 'put people first' traditions and values.

But if Labor is to recapture the confidence and majority support of the voting community, we will need to do rather more than even all that. We will have to try and get inside the hearts and minds, and be seen to be doing so, of those millions of ordinary working men and women who are bound to see the economic issues affecting them from a rather less grand perspective.

We have to talk, in language that can be understood, to people who feel insecure — about their jobs, about the changing nature of their work, about their wages and conditions, and about the whole unrelenting process of change to which they have been subject over the last decade.

More specifically, we have to *connect* with people:

● who feel vulnerable about their own employment future, because of their perception that there is no such thing any more as a secure permanent job (maybe no less in Australia

than in any other industrialised country, but — here as else-
where — international comparisons do not mean as much as
personal experience)

- who do not necessarily see intuitively how it is that our
  engagement with Asia, and the trade opportunities that flow
  from that, will be of particular relevance to them

- who worry about the employment prospects for their children,
  however much extended education or training is available to
  them

- who know all too well that whatever virtue industry restructuring may have for the economy as a whole, all too often the
  new jobs are not precisely where the old ones were lost, and
  do not involve the same sort of skills

- who see all too clearly the changing nature of work, and in
  particular the disappearance, under technological onslaught,
  of a great many traditional unskilled and semi-skilled jobs

- who may not feel personally confident about their capacity to
  be retrained or learn new skills — or even to find a niche in
  the domestic and community service areas of employment
  which are continuing to expand rapidly

- who may not be confident that they can afford early retirement, or occupy themselves satisfyingly without their days
  being filled with work

- who are unimpressed by the economic virtue of a lower interest rate environment because they are significantly dependent
  for their income on interest from investments, or

- who may just *feel* less well off in a low inflation environment,
  simply because there are less new dollars going to their pay
  packets or home valuations: it may be 'money illusion' for
  the economists, but for many ordinary Australians that illusion is very real.

So the challenge of economic policy for Labor now, in opposition, is not only to articulate and act in the Parliament, on the

big macro-policy issues of the day, in accordance with clear, economically defensible and equitable principles. It is to be systematically working away at a whole range of micro-policy issues related to the future of work; the regional and local impact of structural reform, including competition policy; retirement incomes; lifetime education and training; satisfying and dignified 'third-age' occupations — and all the other very specific issues that do matter to ordinary working Australians.

Unless we do care, and are seen to be caring, about the things that matter to people, we cannot complain if they in turn do not care very much about what happens to us.

Chapter 4

A Budget of Betrayal

Kim Beazley

We are a more creative nation than the Liberal's budget recognises or permits. We are a more united community than this budget will encourage.

We are a nation of greater integrity than the shattered election pledges this budget contains. Pledges that were given so forcefully and in such an unqualified manner by John Howard only a few months ago.

This is a budget of betrayal. Not just the betrayal of election promises. But the betrayal of the Australian promise itself — the promise of Australia working towards a more fair, a more just, a more inclusive and united society. The message of this budget is don't be sick; don't be old; don't expect to go to university; if you're unemployed, too bad; and if you're young and unemployed, forget it.

Last election John Howard told Australians they could trust him. He told Australians that whatever budget numbers he inherited, all promises would be delivered. This budget breaches that trust. A long list of broken promises. Promises made to mainstream Australia and made to battlers. Promises made to students. Promises made to the elderly. Promises made to the state and local governments. No contrived dribbling out of bad news for mainstream Australia and the battlers prior to the budget's presentation can hide that fact.

The new morality of this government is that there are core promises made and non-core promises, although no such distinction was made before the election. Core honesty; non-core honesty. Would you take that from your children?

John Howard inherited an economy that he said 'was better than good'. Indeed he did. One with inflation that had been averaging 2.5 per cent. An economy that had been growing 4 per cent a year. One which created 700 000 jobs over the last three years. One which saw our exports, particularly those of manufactured goods, grow and diversify.

He inherited an economy with a very small public sector by international standards and a budget outcome better than any in the industrialised world, bar a couple. Compare all that with the economy we inherited back when we came into government — unemployment and inflation over 10 per cent, and a $25 billion budget deficit in today's dollars.

This government placed a dead hand on the economy when they took office. A 'core' reality of this budget is that the dead hand is still there, so much so that the Treasury officials have observed in the Budget Papers that 'possible confidence effects, while significant, do not fully offset the direct short-term effects of the measures, resulting in a small net contractionary impact on activity in 1996–97'. That's Treasury-speak for saying that this budget not only does nothing for growth — it will reduce it.

Instead of undermining growth, the government should be promoting it. And with more growth the budget could be restored to balance without the need for savage cuts to valuable public programs. Higher growth destroys the case for savage budget cuts. By keeping growth up — by aiming for sustainable growth at the 4 per cent we averaged during the last four years in office — we also bring unemployment down. And unemployment, not the budget, is the number one problem facing Australia.

The Treasurer says that saving is our number one problem. We have no argument that Australia has long had a saving problem — and we did more to solve it, with the introduction of our national superannuation scheme, than any previous government. And now Mr Costello places a huge question mark over that achievement.

We have no argument that Australia's longer term economic interests are well served by restoring the budget to balance —

that is why we, alone among post-war Australian governments, delivered successive surpluses in the late 1980s. But we say the best way to restore the budget to balance is through a moderate program of budget cuts, over the whole life of this Parliament, which does not harm valuable public programs, and which does-not harm growth and which provides hope rather than despair for the jobless.

Mr. Costello makes a virtue of the fact that this budget holds growth back so that in three years time, and with massive budget cuts, the surplus will be $1 billion.

It suits the government to have low growth because low growth makes it appear as if bigger cuts are needed to restore the budget to balance. But with average growth close to 4 per cent it would be possible to achieve balance without savage budget cuts. On the government's own admission, these cuts are not necessary to reduce the debt ratio: that would have happened anyway. And so far as reduction of that current account deficit is concerned, that is hardly going to change in 1997.

These cuts are not being made for genuine reasons of economic necessity. They are being made to satisfy the Liberals' ideological obsession with reducing the role of government in Australian society. Significantly, the burdens in this budget are not equally shared.

It is a wrong-headed interpretation of this budget that it soaks the rich as well as the poor. Mr Costello has leapt to the challenge of the tax commissioner to collect $800 million of avoided tax by the wealthiest Australians with a slash of his feather duster; $100 million and a bit of a look. Hopefully it will be collected voluntarily, he said. And have a bit of health insurance while you're at it, he invites wealthy Australians, or we'll give you a little snip of a levy.

The burden is borne by the battlers, the job seekers, the students, the elderly and middle-income Australia. He offers tax cuts. For a dual income family earning up to a total of $79 000, these tax cuts amount to $3.85 a week for each dependant child.

But families want to educate their children. They want to use child care. They are worried about their kids getting an opportunity to work. They want to know that if their elderly parents need a nursing home bed, they will be able to afford it. They use public hospitals. They carry the burden of increased taxes and charges when the states funds are slashed.

Under successive Labor governments a generation of women has grown up with new expectations and hopes for the future. Meaningful employment, on-going careers — a totally different world from that of their mothers and grandmothers. The female labour force is over 50 per cent larger today than it was in 1983. The prime minister shows no sign of recognising this fact. But this fact is why successive Labor governments made available, affordable, high-quality child care. This recognised that many families do not have the means to allow one partner to leave the workforce to care for children, even if they would like to.

At the last election the Liberals were at pains to promise that this quality child care — available and affordable on an equal basis to all Australians — would remain. But what do we find in the budget?

We find a range of mean-spirited measures which make child care more expensive for all families. For those using community based care it will be $14 per child per week more. And this will not be all; $500 million is taken out of child care and it will be the parents who make up the difference.

Families contain people of all ages. What does this budget do for families of older Australians? We see a proposal which may force older Australians who need nursing home care, or their children, to find around $26 000 in entry fees. Nursing home residents also face a new daily fee of up to $34 per day, or $12 000 per year,depending on their income. Mr Howard says that children should pay for their elderly parents to have a nursing home bed. This is yet another way this government is getting families to pay more.

But it gets worse. Many older families, frail but still living in their own homes, are dependant on the services, such as Meals on Wheels, provided by the Home and Community Care (HACC) program. These families are to be stung by greatly increased user fees. That's code for increased charges for Meals on Wheels and the like.

The prime minister gives with one hand and takes away even more with the other. Like a man that comes up to you in the street and says 'here's $5, now give me $7'.

Health

In the health area Mr Howard promised to 'retain Medicare in its entirety' and to provide a net increase in health funding. Instead, we have indirect cuts through reductions in the Financial Assistance Grants to the states, and direct cuts to Hospital Funding Grants. The combined effect is a cut of around $800 million dollars over four years.

The nastiest if not the largest of the government's health cuts is the abolition of the Commonwealth Dental Health Program. This program, which spends around $110 million a year, is exclusively directed at the provision of basic and emergency dental services to health card holders. The abolition of this program will reproduce the two-to-three-year waiting lists which prompted the Commonwealth's intervention and which the program has substantially reduced.

The budget speech contained the following explanation for the cuts, 'as waiting times for the public dental health services have now been reduced, funding for the Commonwealth Dental Health Program will cease...' As if your teeth can be fixed once and that is the only time you need a dentist!

Another of the Coalition's major betrayals in health is big increases in the costs of prescription drugs. For a family with three children — and we all know how often they get sick at once — at $20 a script, that's $60 for the family, for just one visit to the chemist. And the increased pharmaceutical charge for pensioners breaks Mr Howard's explicit promise to 'maintain the real value of all pension benefits and other entitlements for low income earners'.

But above all, there is the threat to bulk billing. The government says that it will maintain it, yet eliminates the CPI adjustment to doctors fees. Bulk billing is voluntary. Hundreds of doctors will stop bulk billing with this change. With another budget next May, you just have to wonder how many more changes, and how many fee increases there are going to be.

Regions

We do not equally share the burden of this Budget. Those who live in regional Australia carry it disproportionately. Regional communities have already been hit by a round of cuts. Many centres have lost their CES and Tax offices. And now they lose their local Medicare offices, and they will pay more for the services that continue.

During the recent election the Coalition asserted that regional communities were 'Australia's forgotten people' and promised to 'Revitalise Regional Australia'. Betrayal has been as swift as it is comprehensive. This government has abandoned regional Australia. In common with its approach to other issues of national importance, it has abandoned its responsibilities to lead, to coordinate and to cooperate with the people of Australia's heartland.

When it comes to regional Australia, this Coalition has quickly become a government in exile. They are absentee landlords with a big city focus — a government of capital city lawyers from leafy suburbs.

Roads are regional Australia's vital arteries; something city dwellers often forget. Road funding through the National Highway System has been slashed by $620 million. Even with the Pacific Highway and Black Spots programs, total road funding to the regions has been *cut* by $150 million over the next three years, and will be hit with an additional $45 million cut the year after that.

Infrastructure projects in centres such as Townsville, Moe and Newcastle, with a total value of $150 million, have been community-building cooperation between business, all levels of government, local communities and unions, that had become the hallmark of regional development under Labor.

Savage cuts to education spending and labour market programs will have a more than proportional impact in regional Australia. It is no wonder that the government's document 'Rebuilding Regional Australia' makes no direct mention of education. Universities mean jobs and wages in regional areas. The impact of these education cuts on regional economies is huge. Yet this government intends to cut the funding for regional universities for every campus in every region in every state.

Slashing labour market programs will have a punitive impact on both regional unemployed and the local government authorities and organisations that have benefited from the programs under Labor.

The ABC will not be able to insulate regional Australia from the massive cuts. National sporting events, news, current affairs, vital local weather and radio services for rural and regional Australians are threatened by Mr Howard's decision to cut $65 million from the nation's public broadcaster.

Mr Fischer and his National Party have willingly collaborated with the Liberals in the betrayal of what they would have us believe is their constituency. These people are over-represented in a ministry which they would have us believe is their constituency. These people are over-represented in a ministry in which they lack the clout to stand up to ignorant Liberal colleagues and defend the interests of regional Australia. They deserve to share the retribution that awaits Liberals in regional seats at the next election.

Education

The proposals for education deserve outright condemnation, not only because they cut off resources but also because they show the barrenness and prejudice in what passes for vision by this government. The government calls them 'farsighted' and 'equitable'. Those who are on the wrong end of them will call them vandalism.

Labor set up and supported one of the most accessible higher education systems in the world. The government proposes to take so much funding out of universities that they will be harmed for years. Look at what this budget has done to young people and their parents, and their expectations. Labor brought higher education within the reach of all young people in Australia, wherever they lived, whatever their circumstances.

This has gone. If you or your parents are well-off, you're OK. If not, you're not. This vandalism goes on in school and vocational education. Funding for schools will be cut, including resources for capital and literacy programs. Assistance for students with disabilities will be stopped altogether. Vocational education will be cut and the government has abandoned its agreement to fund growth in the TAFE system.

And remember this: We've crossed a line here. Now that universities and schools and TAFE are just other sources of revenue, who can be confident that there is not more of this to come? It's on for young and old. Mr Howard has asked us to mortgage our children's university education. And he has told us to mortgage our old age accommodation.

Industry

This government has abdicated its responsibilities to Australian industry.

Think of an industry where Australians have moved to the cutting edge, think of an industry that has made the hard yards in improved productivity and export competitiveness, think of key growth areas for small business, and you will be thinking of some sector, enterprise or activity that has been damaged in this budget. They fail to comprehend the fact that innovative export oriented industries are central to any strategy for future prosperity and jobs growth.

Their treatment of the Australian Made Campaign is a powerful sign of the extent to which they have lost the plot. The green and gold logo symbolised the emerging hope for the future of Australian industry, and the government has strangled it.

This budget does not slash programs to end rorts, it hacks away at success stories, and punishes innovators. Support for the manufacturing sector is to be cut by $336 million, or 60 per cent over the next three years. Exporters whose efforts are crucial to our whole economic future will lose $500 million over the same period.

Industries critical to our export competitiveness and employment growth have been singled out, for example, by the removal of the shipbuilding bounty and the abolition of the computer bounty.

Research and development have been heavily set back by at least a decade. The broken promise that has seen the R & D tax concession cut back will cost industry some $1.25 billion. When combined with the abolition of syndicated research, a total of $2.2 billion will be removed from research and development, to be replaced by a paltry $340 million in grants. The result will see Australian researchers and Australian ideas move offsore, while a range of activities from medical research to information technology and electronics will stall for want of support in this country. Government support for exporters and industry has been crippled by cuts of $100 million from Austrade and $34 million from Ausindustry.

These all represent broken promises. They amount to dishonest government and, just as certainly, they amount to foolish government. Manufacturers, exporters and researchers have been ill served by this budget, and consequently so have we all.

Above all, this budget also betrays the jobless. This is a budget that will commit itself to no jobs targets between now and the end of the century. This budget ends the public labour exchange started by Ben Chifley. It shoves the unemployed into the hands of the inexperienced at the same time that it cuts nearly all of the programs that made the long-term unemployed job-ready.

Sheer, ignorant prejudice has meant that the Coalition has torn down the highly successful Working Nation employment and training programs. The very programs that were regularly praised by both major employers groups and individual Australians assisted back into the workforce.

And do not think that unemployment is not a mainstream issue. Three decades of technological change and industrial restructuring have meant that many have experienced the shock of redundancy, previously only experienced by few. Since the election of the Howard government redundancy has been legion in the public sector, in Telstra, and in a wide range of industries.

Australians expect their prime ministers to stand up for the weak and forgotten. To stand above treasurers and a desire to please the financial markets, when necessity dictates. To have a sense of community. The unemployed, Aboriginals, the young, the aged, have always needed it. For Mr Costello's budget, this prime minister stood aside.

Conclusion

This is not a government for communities. It is a government for elite opinion leaders who do not get Meals on Wheels, or use

community child care. Who can afford to pay for tertiary education, dental care, nursing home care. Who will not notice the
burden of higher state taxes and charges.

Australia is a cohesive community. We are an egalitarian
community. Socially just communities are safe communities.
Communities which deny opportunity are in the end denied
security. This government attacks security in public sector
employment, in the safety net when we are out of work, in effective access to public hospitals.

This budget lays down the path to a two-tier society. The
prime minister is driven to division. All that is public, or shared,
is cut and will be cut again. The message is, whatever you can
not pay for, you do not deserve.

It is an old-style Tory budget, scapegoating the battlers and
with a dead hand on the national tiller.

It will be up to business, Australian workers and our community to work their way back to the low inflationary growth
they had and the opportunity we provided. It is a budget whose
poisonous content will gradually seep out.

As a responsible Opposition, Labor will subject its mean-
ness to several tests. Where does a measure betray a promise?
Where does it damage equity? Where does it fail to contribute to
national savings? The community demands no less.

Many measures fail these tests. Many are locked away in the
appropriations legislation, immune in the end to defeat, but not
safe from rigorous criticism in our two Houses.

Others, however, are about revenue raising or go to the
heart of community entitlement programs. The government's
measures on the Higher Education Charges, on Nursing Homes
contributions and charges, and Pharmaceutical Benefits for
pensioners and families, for example, can be rigorously
opposed. We will oppose them.

This prime minister was elected promising Australians that
they could be 'comfortable and relaxed' and that he would make
their lives more secure. Instead he has hit them with massive
changes, making their lives less secure. He promised a zone of
comfort, but has delivered a nation more fearful than ever.

Australians now face changes they do not need — changes
that hit the family budget and will divide communities. This

budget is a mere irritant for the rich, but a disaster for the disadvantaged, and a matter of despair for the unemployed.

It is the first chapter in the story of a new, unfair Australia. For all those who had hoped for a secure future for themselves and their children, this is a budget of betrayal.

Chapter 5

Social Inclusiveness in an Open Economy

Mark Latham

Several years after Labor in government experienced its first great rout at a federal election, Jim Scullin was asked if he would write the memoirs of his administration. 'It nearly killed me to live through it', he replied; 'it would kill me to write about it'.

Today most of us are in better shape; and part of the reason is that Labor has developed a political culture which values ideas and policy creation.

In 1931 R. S. Ross (Lloyd's father) lamented that 'we, as a party, in Australia write no books, produce no pamphlets and set up no research'. A generation of true believers had to await the Fabian renaissance of the 1960s to correct this shortcoming.

Since then, of course, Labor has not looked back. Each of the advances in Australian public policy in my lifetime have been Labor's advances: Gough Whitlam's program of social democracy, Paul Keating's renovation of the economy, Brian Howe's modernisation of social policy.

Australian politics has long followed a cycle of initiative and reaction: Labor advancing its reform agenda; the dead hand of the Coalition trying to smother it.

The Liberal Party has always known what it opposes, but rarely what it favours. Socialism, welfarism, feminism, republicanism — these days it even opposes liberalism, at least in the classical sense.

For all the criticisms we have and will level at John Howard, the common theme is this: he has no answers to the core tensions facing an open society and open economy:

- how to provide economic security without diminishing international competitiveness

- how to achieve full employment and overcome the tendency of a globalised economy to exclude a significant number of citizens from the production process

- how to fund the active role of government off an internationally competitive tax base

- how to adapt the welfare state to a post-industrial era which demands far greater customisation and flexibility in service delivery

- how to create new sources of social stability which replenish the strength and coherence of civil society.

In this respect the ball is already back in Labor's court. Our electoral success for the remainder of this decade will in large part depend on how effectively we add value and ideas to the public debate. How we provide answers to these core issues.

In the continuum of Australian politics it was ever thus: Menzies' neglect — Whitlam's program — Fraser's malaise — Keating's big picture — Howard's inadequacies — new Labor initiatives.

Putting aside the lost hope and disappointment of 2 March, we would not have it any other way.

Whenever I think of Labor's role:

- as the grand old party of Australian politics

- our capacity to survive the worst splits within and defeats without

- the constant pressure to renew and revitalise Labor policy,

I think of the old Yiddish story of the man waiting at the city gates for the millennium: 'Big job', he said, 'but at least the work is steady'.

Our work in Opposition should start with the first issue I mentioned: economic security.

Economic security

A defining feature of an open economy is uncertainty. For workers without internationally competitive skills this translates into economic insecurity.

New patterns of technology, skills and investment have lifted the pace of economic restructuring. What used to be known as steady jobs are now subject to multiskilling and continuous change.

While in government we presented these changes as an opportunity for the nation; for many workers they represent a threat. This is the basic lesson of the Keating years: economic change and internationalisation can be as threatening for citizens in the workforce as those outside it. Our safety net needs to include workers as much as it protects people — the aged, sick and unemployed — excluded from the production process.

The emergence of a global, post-Fordist economy — in which the skills and capability of citizens varies widely — is forcing left-of-centre parties like ours to recast their core values and appeal. Let me explain.

Out of the Industrial Revolution, which harnessed machine power for commercial purposes, politics came to be defined around ownership issues. The owners of capital were said to be exploiting those who worked the machines. Questions of equality and worker representation were understood and argued out within this framework of owners and non-owners.

In the post-industrial era, however, economic opportunity is being defined as much by access to human capital as physical capital. Indeed, in many cases, the traditional divide between capital and labour has been blurred.[1]

The labour market bargaining power of highly skilled, internationally competitive labour — the so-called 'knowledge workers' — often exceeds that of the owners of capital. Hence, in an open economy not all workers are vulnerable, at least not in the sense of having their labour exploited.

In Australia up to 30 per cent of the labour force features

internationally competitive skills, contributing successfully to enterprises in the traded sector. These highly skilled workers — Robert Reich has labelled them symbolic analysts — have been the major beneficiaries of nineteen successive quarters of national economic growth. They have accumulated assets and wealth previously unknown to 'ordinary' workers (and, along the way, given much greater credit to their own industry and skills than the policies of the former government).

Conversely, the majority of Australian workers do not exercise internationally competitive skills. In an open labour market — where the supply of labour outstrips demand — these semi-skilled, lower productivity workers, mostly engaged in the non-traded sector, lack the bargaining strength to secure real wage increases and take a share of national economic growth.

This demonstrates the way in which globalisation is associated with new forms of inequity and social exclusion. A new layer of income inequality has emerged in Australia, directly linked to the value labour adds to the internationalised production system. As a nation's economy becomes more open, income relativities move closer to those of its trading partners. Low productivity workers do not directly share in the new sources of national income generated out of free trade and investment.

Hence economic and political interests in Australia have been redefined. I would argue, for instance, that the economic interests of semi-skilled, blue-collar workers now have more in common with a small retailer (technically, an owner of capital) in the main street of Werribee than a multimedia specialist (technically, part of the labour force) working in South Yarra.

Obviously, in Opposition Labor needs to redefine and clarify its core constituency. I offer this starting point: a party which represents workers, citizens and locations which, if it were not for the active role of the public sector, would be overwhelmed by free market forces. That is, semi-skilled and unskilled workers, local service providers, tradespeople, contractors and franchise holders; plus those excluded from a productive place in our open economy.

Already the Howard government has shown that it is not

willing to fund the public cost of distance and isolation. John Sharp's announcement on 17 July that 'there is no clear rationale or constitutional basis for Commonwealth involvement (in regional development)' is part of a clearance sale in National Party tradition and relevance.

This is a defining issue in Australian politics. In a big country like ours it cannot be assumed that economic resources are fully mobile. Distance often makes markets dysfunctional. This is why the public sector plays a special role in regional Australia (the bush, provincial towns and outer urban areas) — providing jobs, services and opportunities which the private sector will not provide due to the tyranny and costs of distance. Rural and regional Australia have formed a starting point for Labor's defence of the active role of government.

Most of all, Labor needs to confirm its credentials as a party protecting workers against the inequality and insecurity of globalisation. This is a snapshot of the new middle ground of Australian politics: families juggling work and parenting responsibilities, highly geared mortgages,[2] hand-to-mouth living standards, workers struggling to secure productivity-based wage increases.

Of the many depressing statistics from the last election the one which worries me most concerns the 40 per cent of federal electorates with the highest proportion of double income families. We now hold just 13 of these 60 seats.[3] That is, the Labor Party, which was formed to protect the interests of workers, has lost the support of families which (on the official data) do the most work.

A Labor Party without the majority support of these workers is a party in need of change. While each of us can be proud of our achievements in government, they alone will not win seats at the next election.

History tells us that whenever Labor has lost heavily it has had to reinvent itself to regain office. The party which won the 1972 election was very different from that which lost in 1996. So too between 1983 and 1975. Hence this is not a time for letting our pride about the past blind us to the changes Labor needs to make post-1996.

Social inclusiveness

An odd thing about our term of government was the way in which Labor gained a reputation for doing things at either end of the political spectrum. At one extreme we were seen as agents of economic change, opening up new opportunities for capital and trade. At the other end, we were regarded as doing things for people primarily outside the production system.

This reputation is essentially an issue of relevance. It is not possible in Australia to sustain an electoral majority by promoting market forces at one end of the spectrum and the social safety net at the other. What the election result showed is that we need something in between.

Labor needs to look above as well as below the safety net for a full understanding of social inclusiveness. This means rethinking some of the basic principles of social democracy.

In a post-industrial economy variations in skill levels have become the main determinant of lifetime opportunities. This challenges the key assumption on which the welfare state was established: that governments could meet the standardised needs of citizens through the provision of universal freedoms (defined as rights) and universal entitlements to a material standard of living.

Now, however, it can be seen that the skill requirements and capability threshold of each individual are unique. Governments can no longer assume, particularly with their mass production of services and entitlements, that one size fits all.

Hence the segmentation of government into a series of programs which correspond with part-of-life characteristics — race, gender, age and so on — is no longer an effective way to deal with the circumstances and skill requirements of each individual. If people have problems which require the assistance of the public sector, they most likely cut across these segments. A poor education, unemployment, access issues and various forms of discrimination often overlap and reinforce each other. Just as socio-economic disadvantage is a whole-of-life experience, the public sector needs to develop whole-of-government solutions.

It is increasingly difficult for governments to generalise about the causes of skill deficiency. For instance, equity

programs for higher education in Australia assume an inade-
quate level of access for non-English-speaking background
(NESB) people, particularly newly arrived migrants. In practice,
however, given the diversity of parenting and work ethics
among different cultural groups, young NESB people have
higher participation rates than English-speaking-background
people. In many cases, such as Chinese, Korean and Vietnamese
speakers, the level of participation is strikingly high.[4] I would
argue that governments no longer give their best support to
multiculturalism (itself based on the virtues of diversity)
through monolithic programs and categories which, in their
delivery, end up defying diversity.

Labor's definition of social inclusiveness should not seek to
break society into a set of categories disconnected from socio-
economic circumstances. Perversely enough, in the popular culture, this builds a perception of exclusivity in access programs
and safety net services. Labor's starting point must be socio-
economic status and capability, not a loose assumption that
people sharing a specific characteristic also share the same
access to economic and social resources. The public sector
should be about solving the problems of disadvantage and
poverty in a customised way, without the folly of standardisation. One size or category no longer fits all.

Social democrats can no longer assume that systems of pas-
sive welfare universally create the basis of active citizenship.
Much more is needed to restore the legitimacy and effectiveness
of the welfare state — customisation, flexibility and a strong
sense of reciprocal responsibilities.

Social democracy has always structured itself like a fortress:
people need to be able to unlock the gates or scale the walls
before they can enjoy its benefits. Those of us who believe in the
active role of government need to build ladders to a post-Fordist
welfare state.

Time sequencing

Indeed the welfare system has a critical role to play in delivering economic security. In its present form it does not cope well
with wide fluctuations in economic circumstances. By and large,

it offers a steady sequence of transfer payments, with little capacity for bringing forward or deferring benefits according to personal need.

This is why transfer payments need to be time sequenced against uncertainty. That is, given the flexibility by which citizens can adjust their entitlements against the contingencies of economic and lifestyle change.

Let me give an example. It should be possible to establish a parenting account which bundles together the prospective entitlements of a family in child endowment, child care benefits and schooling. Within prudential limits, parents would be able to draw forward or defer their entitlements according to family circumstances.

If one partner, for instance, suffered a reduction in earnings they might seek an advance on child-care resources to allow the other parent to seek work. Or, if the parents were uncomfortable with out-of-home child care, they might defer that part of their account to cover schooling costs.

Mandated superannuation schemes also have potential for time sequencing. The super pool in Australia should be seen and developed as an anchor against the uncertainties of economic change. Citizens would be able to draw on their forward savings to advance their immediate welfare in labour market retraining, housing relocation, supplementary income and the other costs of economic adjustment.

In this fashion time sequencing not only fosters economic security but also the customisation of entitlements. It allows recipients to mould their benefits to suit personal circumstances rather than be locked into rigid departmental guidelines and categories. This sense of ownership and control has the potential to improve public confidence in the tax–transfer system.

Employment creation

In most Western nations it is now possible to talk of a 30–40–30 society — 30 per cent of citizens with competitive skills, high productivity and growing incomes; another 40 per cent who — while in work — face the economic insecurity of restricted employment tenure and earning capacity; plus a bottom 30 per cent of unemployed, chronically ill and other economically inactive citizens.[5] Social democracy is still searching for answers to the core inequities of this new social structure.

Australian Labor's period in office points to some important lessons on economic policy. We now have first hand experience with the myths of the competitive advantage paradigm — the belief that supply side reforms optimise economic outcomes. In truth, all the micro reforms and competition policies under the sun will still exclude a significant proportion of citizens and locations from an active role in an internationalised economy.

The impact of economic restructuring is uneven at a local level. The growth of new industries and jobs rarely matches the location and skills of jobs lost in sectors previously excluded from micro reform. Orthodox adjustment packages — relying on sectoral plans, subsidies and reskilling — while themselves useful, have not been able to compensate for a loss of employment demand. Governments need to develop new forms of intervention on the demand side of regional labour markets to ensure that labour force skills correspond to the creation of suitable work.

This type of public sector employment creation has become critical with the disappearing middle of the Australian labour market.[6] The changing nature of work in the services sector is now replicating the experience in manufacturing, with the elimination of large numbers of semi-skilled jobs. While economists have always argued, in the long cycle of economic growth, that job numbers lost in old industries are ultimately replaced by new sector employment, the current changes are distinctive in two key ways.

First, post-Fordist work reflects a much higher plane of skill level in the production process. The replacement of standardised, physical labour with knowledge work has obvious features of exclusivity in the labour market. Second, forseeable job replacement effects — which are arising primarily from the outsourcing of household functions[7] — display aspects of locational imbalance.

Material benefits and lifestyles are increasingly being determined by a person's contribution to internationally exposed production processes. High incomes bring with them access to high cost housing areas and also a high propensity for outsourcing household consumption. In this fashion, high skill locations enjoy a virtuous cycle of high income, high consumption and high employment. By contrast, low skill areas are locked into a cycle of low consumption and low employment. Successful individuals usually move out of these areas while new, poorly skilled residents move in, producing an urban churning effect.

These problems of exclusivity in skill formation and regional employment lie outside the scope of orthodox economic theory. They do not form part of the competitive advantage paradigm or Treasury's econometric model. They will not be part of the Howard government's thought process, let alone policy.

Labor in Opposition needs to explore new paradigms to cope with this issue. Jeremy Rifkin's work[8] offers a useful starting point — the argument that the public sector should fund the outsourcing of civil society functions as a new (socially useful) sector of semi-skilled employment.

For all the analysis of the East Asian economic miracle, little attention has been given to the role of public sector employment in these economies. The city-state of Singapore, for instance, is best known for each of the virtues of traded competitiveness: high value-adding and productivity; personal thrift and savings; and comprehensive global integration. Yet Singapore also has a small army of public employees undertaking valuable work in the non-traded sector: particularly in civic maintenance, gardening and public health.

This type of standardised, semi-skilled work out of the public sector is an essential part of the attainment of full employment in an open economy. It actively compensates for the loss of comparable jobs in other parts of the economy. It matches skill levels across the labour force (which, despite the best training initiatives, can never reach full flexibility) against the availability of skill-suited work.

Gain sharing

Another lesson of the Keating years is the need for Labor to formalise a gain–sharing model on living standards. That is, how to ensure that the industrial relations and tax-transfer systems provide lower productivity workers — the newly insecure 'middle' group in society — with gains in disposable income commensurate with gains in national economic growth.

From the Federation settlement to the opening of the Australian economy in the 1980s, basic wage adjustments and tariff-protected manufacturing put together a loose model for national gain sharing. Economic rents in agriculture and mining were transferred to manufacturing and other urban-based workers.

The major shortcoming of the Accord 1983–96, especially with its ultimate emphasis on retirement income ahead of disposable income, was its failure to formalise an active gain sharing mechanism to the satisfaction of Labor's constituency. While the Party boasted of a record period of national economic growth, the distributional features of GDP did not necessarily lift the living standards of the economically insecure.

It should be remembered, of course, that in its origins the Accord was not designed to cope with the competitive pressures of an open economy or a productivity-based wages system. It was a prices and incomes strategy aimed at breaking the back of inflation by trading money wage increases for social wage gains.

In Opposition Labor needs to develop a gain-sharing model for an open economy. This is an important guarantee against economic insecurity: a guaranteed share of national economic growth for workers without internationally competitive skills. Productivity-based wage bargaining and small safety net adjustments are not enough.

In several parts of the non-traded economy — most notably, the housing construction and road transport sectors — it is difficult to extract labour productivity gains from production systems which already have international best practices (IBP). The only way truck drivers transporting goods from Melbourne to Sydney could increase their productivity would be to bend the law even further. It is not satisfactory under the current system for these IBP workers to be denied decent prospects for steady wage increases. Moreover, the productivity-based system is flawed by the difficulty most service-type workplaces face in even measuring labour productivity.

Political Labor should use the ACTU's living wage submission as a catalyst for its gain-sharing model. That is, to recognise the equity features of a minimum wage based on the living costs of active citizenship in our society.

Importantly, research in the United States has shown that higher minimum wages do not necessarily lead to the overpricing of labour and unemployment. Empirical studies by David Card and Alan Krueger at Princeton University have concluded that:

> minimum wage increases have not had the negative employment effects predicted by the textbook model. Some of the new evidence points toward a positive effect of the minimum wage on employment; most shows no effect at all. Moreover, a re-analysis of previous minimum wage studies finds little support for the prediction that minimum wages reduce employment. If accepted, our findings call into question the standard model of the labour market that has dominated economists' thinking for the past half century.[9]

Given the significance of demand conditions for regional economies, it is not difficult to see the linkage between higher minimum wages and enhanced employment conditions. Studies have consistently shown that patterns of employment by small business are more aligned to demand conditions than supply-side issues like unfair dismissal laws. At least with regard to labour market analysis, Labor can lead the charge against economic correctness.

An economy with a strong traded sector (enjoying the growth potential of high productivity and export penetration) can sustain a strong floor under wage levels in the non-traded sector. This should be the transmission mechanism by which semi-skilled workers receive a decent share of national economic growth. The indexation of the living wage to movements in average earnings would create the basis of income gain-sharing across time. If, as is likely, the Industrial Relations Commission does not entrench these arrangements it would be available to a Federal Labor government to legislate them.

The need for these initiatives has been made more critical by the Howard government's industrial relations agenda. This defines every worker as an individual instead of every workplace as a co-operative enterprise. The introduction of individual employment contracts and removal of collective bargaining strength from the workplace will lead to greater insecurity and inequality for the bottom tier of wage earners. Jeff Borland's research at the University of Melbourne has shown that:

> As one effect of trade unions is to reduce earnings dispersion within the group of employees who are union members, a decrease in union density could affect earnings dispersion. A decline in union density can explain approximately 30 per cent of the increase in variance of earnings of full-time male employees in Australia between 1986 and 1994, and 15 per cent of the increase in the variance of earnings of full-time female employees over the same period.[10]

The membership and bargaining strength of trade unions is an important influence on income equality in the Australian economy. If this declines then a legislated gain-sharing model becomes even more critical for the fairness of our society.

On wages policy Labor's relationship with the trade union movement remains a strategic asset. With the globalisation of capital the usefulness of active fiscal and monetary policies has declined. Wages policy remains the one autonomous macro policy tool still available to national governments. Only unions, as a collective agent in the labour market, can lever wage outcomes in the national interest. Only by agreement with the trade union movement can governments directly influence wage and inflation outcomes.

Otherwise they need to use monetary policy, with earlier and bigger interest rate movements, to pre-emptively strike against a tightening of the labour market. The governor of the Reserve Bank confirmed these fundamentals on 16 July, pointing out that if the bank 'could be more confident that these influences (wage movements in line with low inflation expectations) would win the day, it would be easier for the Bank itself to adjust to low inflation' (that is, ease official interest rates). With the abolition of the Accord process our central bank has lost its security blanket for assessing future wage outcomes.

The Labour movement should never sell short the value of a cooperative agreement between its political and industrial wings. While a replay of the Accord will not be possible — nor, in all its detail, desirable — the ALP and trade union movement should not be reluctant to declare a mutual commitment to:

- establishing a gain-sharing model
- the effective use of macro wages policy
- defending the active role of government and strength of the social wage.

Conclusion

In the television era politics has become more a contest of values than detailed reform programs. This reflects a communications gap between the complexity of political issues in an open society and the restricted means by which most people receive their political information. The medium has tailored the message.

Labor's core values should be security and fairness. We need to talk the language of guarantees — a guaranteed share of national economic growth for low productivity workers; a guaranteed level of employment and public investment in regional Australia; a guarantee that the active role of government can protect workers, citizens and locations from the worst excesses of global competition.

To project these values effectively, however, some things need to change in the party's own political culture. Somewhere in the 1980s we became too civilised and responsible — too much a party of office, not enough a party of crusaders.

If being responsible means putting the profit share ahead of wage increases, Labor needs less of it. If being civilised means patronising the high arts more than public housing estates, Labor needs less of it.

A party like ours runs on passion — people who feel strongly about suffering and injustice. People who want to do something about it. People who see our cause as the great adventure of Australian public life.

Labor is at its best when it mixes its passion for causes with its natural larrikin streak; at its worst when our policy-makers are too scared to put a foot forward for fear of putting a foot wrong.

As a long-serving government we attracted a generation of hangers-on. In Opposition the chattering classes have already started to move on. Some are still lost in the Dandenong Ranges. I think we'll emerge stronger, as a party and a movement, from a period when we are forced to rely much more on each other. Most people who belong to the ALP have made a decision to carry the top weight in public life. Ours is not an easy calling: to have people think well of each other, to believe that understanding and compassion can build a fairer society.

The Tory load is always lighter — to feed off prejudice and ill-will, to assume that people can only advance their interests at the expense of others. This is what the Liberals have always called the natural order of things.

Ultimately time changes most things in politics; yet values and roles can be remarkably constant. The Labor historian Jim Hagan, used these words to describe the party's prospects in New South Wales after our heavy defeat in 1988:

> My father always voted Labor, because he believed that the worst Labor Government was better than any Liberal Government could be. He was often disappointed at what Labor Governments did, but he consoled himself with the belief that the movement was greater than the individual. My father was what sociologists and historians have called class conscious. A consciousness of this kind does not switch off like a light. In the minds of traditional voters, the Labor Party's origins continue in its present history. These origins have to do with protection ... to use the power of government to prevent unemployment, preserve wages and conditions, and protect ordinary folk from the rich and powerful.
>
>   Therein lies hope for the Party. If it can convince its traditional voters that it has renewed its commitment to the fundamental purposes of the Party — and if the Liberal Government demonstrates that it really is worse, then Labor can look forward to the return of traditional support. It would not be the first time that big swings in followed big swings out.

Notes

1   For example, should sub-contractors retain their labour rights for collective bargaining or be subject to business codes outlawing collusive markets?

2   From March 1992 to March 1995 housing debt in Australia rose from $88 billion to $152 billion (72 per cent increase); housing and consumer debt expressed relative to household income rose from 176% to 229%; while household debt relative to the value of all homes rose from 27% to 34.5%. Debt has grown faster than the value of homes, reflecting higher household gearing. Hence household budgets are much more sensitive to mortgage rate movements: from December 1993 to March 1995 interest payments as a proportion of household income rose from 6.8% to 8.5%.

3   Before 2 March the ALP held 28 of these electorates. The 13 remaining are Namadgi, Fraser, Canberra, Sydney, Burke, Jagajaga, Scullin, Greenway, Bruce, Lalor, Werriwa, Melbourne Ports and Holt.

4   See I. Dobson, B. Birrell and V. Rapson, The Participation of Non-English-Speaking-Background Persons in Higher Education, *People and Place*, Vol. 4, No. 1, pp. 46–54.

5   See Will Hutton, High-risk Strategy is Not Paying Off, *Guardian Weekly*, 12 November 1995, p. 13.

6   See B. Gregory and B. Hunter, "The Spatial Structure of the Labour Market", paper presented to the Metropolitan Round Table, 17–18 March 1994, Canberra.

7   Already tourism (outsourcing facilitated by travel) and prepared meals (restaurants, takeaway, home delivery, etc.) have emerged as substantial employment sectors. Other forms of household outsourcing — including child minding, gardening services, pet grooming, home maintenance and security, cleaning, laundering and car repairs — have been gathering strength and are likely to emerge in the next decade as genuine growth sectors. See P. Ruthven, New Growth and Where It's Coming From, *Australian Financial Review*, 5 January 1995, p. 8.

8   J. Rifkin, *The End of Work*, Putnam's Sons, New York, 1995.

9   D. Card and A. Krueger, *Myth and Measurement: The New Economics of the Minimum Wage*, Princeton University Press, 1995, p. 1.

10   J. Borland and R. Wilkins, Earning Inequality in Australia, *The Economic Record*, Vol. 72, No. 216, March 1996, p. 23.

Chapter 6

Building an Inclusive Society

Lindsay Tanner

Labor must commence the process of repositioning itself for a return to government in a world which will be quite different from that left by the Keating government in 1996.

The key themes in this repositioning should be:

- direct intervention to create jobs in regions of high unemployment

- greater commitment to building and renewing infrastructure

- more emphasis on building social institutions rather than cash transfers as a means of creating an inclusive society

- a coherent framework of principles for public ownership, industry assistance and regulation

- new mechanisms for fighting growing market inequality

- more sophisticated research into voter behaviour and aspirations

- greater efforts to reflect Labor's traditional constituencies in our political agenda

- democratising the party, developing ALP members as community participants, and rekindling Labor idealism.

The federal ALP has often been subject to major policy upheavals which have caused great anguish for the party's rank and file at the time. Often the new positions which have emerged have attained widespread acceptance among subsequent generations of Labor supporters. Curtin's adoption of conscription, Whitlam's abandonment of White Australia and acceptance of state aid, and Hawke's floating of the dollar are nowhere near as controversial now as when first introduced.

Such rethinking is usually the product of changing circumstances. The next Labor government will inherit a nation quite different from the one left by the Keating government. The development of a new Labor agenda must therefore be an evolutionary process, capable of accommodating changes in society over the intervening period.

Many Labor supporters automatically associate policy revision with selling out or moving to the Right. It need not necessarily be so. When a shift to the Left occurs it is usually taken for granted, as if the new position is somehow the natural Labor position. Labor members saw the abandonment of the party's uniform land rights position in 1984 as a move to the Right, but few interpreted the 1993 Native Title legislation as a move to the Left.

The task now facing Labor is to build a new policy agenda and political strategy which reflects achievements in government, lessons learned from mistakes, and continuing change in our community.

Changing the message

Our future policy deliberations must reflect the extraordinary changes sweeping through western societies:

- the dramatic impact of internationalisation upon national governments and regulatory frameworks

- the substantial shift in economic power which this has produced, favouring investors, employers and consumers at the expense of borrowers, workers and producers

- the rapid spread of economic insecurity throughout all sections of the community

- the market-driven increase in inequality of wealth and income

- the growing dominance of service industries such as entertainment, leisure, tourism, hospitality and information services

- increasing flexibility in production processes flowing from technological change and work reorganisation

- scarcity of essential resources such as water

- social dislocation and fragmentation associated with problems such as loneliness, low self-esteem and the 'loser' concept.

Labor must seek expression of our core social and egalitarian values in ways which are both politically and economically effective. Our fundamental goals of decent living standards, social equity and economic security remain unchanged. The means of pursuing these goals must change as society changes. This may mean abandoning previous positions, or even reviving earlier approaches previously abandoned.

Creating jobs

Labor in Government was heavily constrained by Treasury ide ology. Supply-side intervention, for instance to improve workers' skills, was permissible. Creating jobs for workers was not. 'Working Nation' devoted billions to training, and very little to actual job creation. With demand for low-skilled jobs in industrial economies plummeting, strong emphasis on skill enhancement is extremely important. Unfortunately it addresses only part of the problem. Without active intervention to help create the right jobs in the right locations, many workers and regions will receive little practical benefit. A future Labor Government should develop job creation strategies in sectors like human services targeted specifically to regions suffering chronically high unemployment.

Building infrastructure

Public sector spending constraints and ideological biases gradu ally squeezed Labor's commitment to infrastructure development, with some notable exceptions such as the One Nation statement. Australia has greater infrastructure needs than most nations because of its size and population distribution. There is no shortage of vital infrastructure work needed, both in building new and renewing existing infrastructure. Quality infrastructure spending creates jobs, enhances regional economic capacity, and delivers political recognition.

Labor's framework of Regional Economic Development organisations and Area Consultative committees had merit, but it relied heavily on the fallacious notion that 'leadership' is the solution to regional economic problems. Leadership is import ant, but it cannot compare with initiatives of serious substance such as the One Nation program of rail-gauge standardisation and port investment. Infrastructure bonds are not the solution: they rely on user-pays arrangements, reduce our capacity to determine national priorities, and are extremely expensive.

Labor governments are great builders. Much of Australia's economic infrastructure and social institutions bear tribute to this. Labor should make infrastructure development, in partnership with regional and local organisations and private companies, a central priority.

Building social institutions

Labor's Social Justice strategy was dominated increasingly by cash payments and 'targeting'. There are signs of growing resentment among people just above the social safety net which may be linked partly to the highly visible nature of cash assistance and the inevitably arbitrary nature of means tests.

Building an inclusive society should depend more on the building of social institutions like Medicare and the Pharmaceutical Benefits Scheme and less on cash transfers. Broadening the Commonwealth Dental Scheme, building more community health centres and legal centres, and strengthening our commitment to public housing are examples of social justice initiatives which could take priority in a future Labor agenda. Locational targeting can help to minimise the risk of high income-earners benefiting unduly from such services. Community institutions in Sunshine and Mill Park do not deal with many clients from Brighton and Kew. Delivering integrated services packages with a strong locational emphasis should be the dominant theme of Labor's inclusive society.

Social justice initiatives should also extend into areas not seen recently in this light. The Commonwealth Bank sale has underlined the absence of any federal government strategy to ensure equitable access to basic financial services for all Australians. Labor should give serious consideration to the concept of 'narrow banking', which separates the provision of traditional consumer banking services from the more complex and speculative functions which have come to dominate the financial services sector.

Intervening intelligently

There is enormous confusion in the community regarding Labor's position on privatisation, regulation and industry assistance. We need a coherent framework around which policy positions on structural economic issues can be developed.

Labor's position on public ownership of particular forms of economic activity should focus on three core issues:

● the universality of use of the product

● the contestability of the market

● the externalities generated by the economic activity.

Selling a government-owned insurance company is acceptable because the market is reasonably contestable, the externalities are of only moderate importance, and the product is not used by everyone. Selling the water supply would be clearly unacceptable: the product is used universally, the externalities are fundamental to human existence, and contestability is very low. These concepts should be regarded as indicative rather than immutable, but it is vital for Labor's credibility that we develop some framework to deal coherently with public ownership issues.

Labor should adopt industry assistance strategies which focus on indirect assistance through enhancement of factors which determine competitiveness, such as research and development, innovation and advanced technology dissemination.

Labor should distance itself from the crude theology of the *Hilmer Report* and develop a much more creative approach to micro-economic reform. In particular, we must restore the central importance of empirical analysis in decision-making. Organisations like the Industry Commission tend to produce reports laden with assertions presented as demonstrable fact yet virtually unsupported by empirical evidence. Labor's competition policy should be determined on a sector by sector basis, should recognise the vital distinction between the trade-exposed and non trade-exposed sectors, and should focus much more on assisting those who are adversely affected by micro-economic reform. Reforms which produce only phoney efficiency gains through wage cuts for workers should be precluded. Labor must also re-examine critically its use of national accounts figures, which reveal less and less about what is actually happening out in real workplaces and real businesses.

Fighting inequality

Inequality is growing alarmingly throughout the industrialised world. Since 1985 the real incomes of the bottom 10 per cent of Australian workers have stagnated while real output per head has grown by 19 per cent (*OECD Employment Outlook 1996*).

As market returns become more unequal and the labor market is gradually deregulated, the importance of this issue will escalate. Fighting inequality is at the very core of Labor's beliefs. The effectiveness of many traditional mechanisms of redistribution is declining, and the need to develop new strategies is fundamental. Options such as a tapered income tax threshold, an earned income tax credit, and weighted tax deductibility for wage and salary payments by companies deserve serious examination. Restructuring the tax system to restrain the growth of market inequality should be a central task for a repositioned Labor Party.

Reordering priorities

Rather than responding only to the efforts of others, Labor should take the lead in raising the profile of emerging national issues. Themes which barely registered in national politics a decade ago will soon play a dominant role in national political debate; themes such as:

- the information technology revolution and the Internet

- the national water crisis

- the social consequences of growing individualism, insecurity and loneliness.

Labor's ability to generate ideas and initiatives in response to such emerging issues will be vital for our political prospects.

Changing the messenger

In spite of many attempts at reform, the Labor Party remains very much an organisation of the 1970s. Restructuring our policies and priorities will count for little if we are unable to reform the means by which these objectives are pursued.

Understanding our constituency

Labor first discovered the importance of opinion polling in the early 1970s under the influence of Mick Young. Since that time our use of such research techniques has not changed much. Labor is long overdue for the next quantum leap in research into political opinion and behaviour. Our focus is still limited to the next election, we make little effort to understand factors which form long-term voter allegiance and factors which disrupt it, and we have only just begun to structure our polling longitudinally.

Data in the Australian Election Study and associated analysis by academics Clive Bean (ANU) and Ian McAllister (Manchester University) give some indication of the path Labor should follow. The recent AES insights include:

- the extent of voter identification with the Labor and conservative parties has dropped from 91 per cent to 78 per cent since 1987

- the proportion of the electorate which always votes for the same party has declined from 60 per cent to 52 per cent since 1987

- at the 1996 federal election, the Labor share of the votes of Asian-born migrants was 25 percentage points higher than Labor's share of the Australian-born vote

- there is still a significant gender gap, with roughly 5 per cent fewer women voting Labor than men

- the proportion of the electorate which is self-employed or which has a head of household who is self-employed has more than doubled since 1979 to 20 per cent

- in 1996 for the first time, the number of 'post-materialists' (voters predominantly interested in broader quality of life issues) exceeded the number of 'materialists' (voters predominantly interested in material economic issues directly affecting them).

These are merely initial glimpses of some of the underlying electoral phenomena which Labor needs to study. What factors form the political allegiances of new voters? How strong are their loyalties? What factors might change them? How important are factors like class, gender, ethnicity, life-stage and region? How meaningful are short-term poll outcomes on voting intention, leader popularity and issue importance?

Polling and focus group research is expensive, and Labor's resources are limited. Yet if we fail to understand fully the factors motivating voter behaviour our efforts to develop a strategy to return to government will be based largely on groping in the dark.

Restraining the new elite

Labor's doctrine is now dominated by the world-view of the tertiary educated generation of the 1970s, a group to which I belong. This group contains two distinct elements: those with a history of some political activity, who tend to be socially progressive and economically agnostic, and those who focused on getting their degrees and jobs, who tend to be economically libertarian and socially agnostic. The Keating government agenda of deregulation, internationalisation, multiculturalism and Aboriginal reconciliation was dominated by this generation's outlook.

Unfortunately much of the rest of Australia, including large sections of Labor's base, does not share these views. They no longer merely tolerate or ignore these themes: in the 1996 federal election many actively rebelled against them.

The growing dominance of these perspectives is international and almost irresistible. They reflect the rise of the services economy, increasing affluence and massive growth in tertiary education. They are producing new fault-lines in Australian politics, which are not reflected by existing divisions between the major parties. This presents enormous challenges to Labor. Its hold on its newer constituency is under threat from the Democrats and the Greens, but its efforts to resist this threat tend to endanger its hold on the allegiance of its old constituency. The troubles of the New Zealand Labour Party are a stern reminder of how serious such problems can become.

There is no easy solution to this growing contradiction because the perspectives of the two constituencies are so different. This will change eventually, but Labor has to ensure that it offers a balanced agenda or risk permanently alienating substantial sections of its base support. Careful scrutiny of Labor's language, culture and focus will not dissolve these divisions, but it may help Labor to be more inclusive and reflective of all its various constituencies.

Rekindling idealism

The Labor Party is not accustomed to success. The unparalleled success of the 1980s brought with it some unfortunate changes in Labor culture. In particular, there are many signs of a growing carpetbagger tendency. With Labor governments controlling a wide range of jobs and career opportunities, ALP membership became for some a career move rather than a commitment.

The latest edition of the Young Labor Network's newsletter has most of its third page devoted to a list of 'Networkers' who have recently got jobs working for right-wing Labor politicians. It is headed 'Congratulations', and conveys a rather obvious message: the central objective of ALP involvement is career enhancement. When the involvement of young people in the ALP is kindled by career aspirations rather than idealism the party has a good deal to be concerned about.

This problem partly reflects the professionalisation of politics since the 1970s, but it must be addressed nevertheless. Labor must ensure that the idealism of 'the light on the hill' is not swamped completely by ambition and cynicism.

Developing members

The ALP hardly devotes any resources to developing its membership, in contrast to parties like the British Labour Party. Our membership is an underdeveloped and under-utilised resource. ALP membership is a very frustrating and unrewarding experience for many party members.

Emerging political parties around the world, often peddling quite extreme platforms, are building political success on grassroots community activity.

By participating in community activities, helping people solve local problems, and working on practical grassroots issues, party members have built extremely strong bases of political support.

Australians tend to see politics as a process of getting elected and governing, or campaigning on a single issue. The notion of active community involvement as a foundation for political activity is not widely accepted. Yet the consequences of this non-involvement can be seen very starkly in the 1996 Victorian election results.

Such a major refocusing of the party membership's activities is a big project, but it could reap substantial rewards. As the base of loyal Labor voters continues to shrink, building and maintaining networks of community support will be increasingly important. Labor can no longer afford to treat party membership as a minor part of its overall strategy.

Democratising the party

A central aspect of mobilising our membership is to provide members with a much more substantial involvement in decision-making. ALP structures in most states are nowhere near as open or democratic as those of most trade unions. Members are not allowed to elect key party office-holders, policy development processes are often inaccessible, and power is too concentrated at the highest levels of the party.

Sporadic reforms have occurred over the past five years, but there is still a long way to go. Labor must connect its membership with its power structures, while it still enjoys the benefits of the two-party system.

Repositioning Labor need not involve heart-wrenching reversals which devastate the commitment of a generation of party supporters. It does not mean that we have to accept the Liberals' agenda. It does require us to rethink some of our basic assumptions about how we go about achieving our objectives. With a constructive and thoughtful reassessment of our approach, Labor can adapt to the structural changes occurring within Australian society and re-emerge as the natural party of the majority of Australians.

Chapter 7

Rebuilding Labor:
Communicating our Values

Martin Ferguson

I am the representative of a traditional Labor electorate — the federal seat of Batman. Steeped as I am in the history and traditions of the great Australian labor movement, I understand what an honour, privilege and duty it is to represent this constituency. I am the tenth member for the federal seat of Batman since it was proclaimed in 1906. In those ninety years my constituents have only twice returned a non-Labor MP to stand in the House of Representatives. My predecessor was Brian Howe.

The people of Batman have remained loyal to Labor because they understand the essential values of our party to stand up for the have-nots, to redress the balance and to build a more egalitarian society. They back Labor because they know it is the only political force which not only keeps up the struggle for a fair share of the cake but also will deliver those fair shares.

While my constituents maintain their faith in Labor, it is obvious that a large number of our fellow Australians unfortunately do not have the same commitment. This means that a considerable rethinking and redefining of the Labor role is needed by all sections of the labor movement. As a new member of the Labor Caucus, I want to become an active part of that redefining, that rethinking of our policy — rethinking what it means to be Labor in the twenty-first century.

But before I come to that, I would like to discuss my first commitment in my first term as a Labor member of Parliament.

That commitment will be to the people of Batman, an inner metropolitan Melbourne electorate which has for many years relied on a manufacturing industry base that is now disappearing. The suburbs in the electorate include Alphington, Bundoora, Coburg North, Croxton, Fairfield, Northcote, Preston, Regent, Reservoir, Thornbury and Westgarth.

The people of the electorate are working people whose priorities for their families are better job opportunities, better housing opportunities, better educational opportunities, better health opportunities and support for the aged. A comparatively high number of people in my constituency are unemployed due to industry restructuring. Those in jobs tend to be unskilled, low-skilled or in traditional blue-collar trades. Nearly half of my constituents speak a language other than English at home and one in ten are not fluent in English.

I promised my constituents that I would commit myself to one major objective in my first term: to create new jobs, more jobs and better jobs for our community. Not only do I want to keep companies such as Kodak, Diana Ferrari, CSIRO, Howe Leather and Flair suits viable in my electorate, I want to help these and other companies in the Batman electorate expand to create extra jobs for my constituents.

I also appreciate the importance of small business in my electorate, with almost 70 per cent of all jobs created under Labor being in the small business sector. Importantly, I believe that the local community, business, unions and higher education institutions — such as RMIT and La Trobe University — can together attract new employers and develop new job opportunities for Melbourne's north in high tech, education, health care and tourism. It is also very important that we now have in place the newly democratically elected Darebin City Council. The councillors, the local state MPs and I are already cooperating with other organisations and individuals in what is the most important role that we all have as representatives of our constituency — creating jobs.

As president of the ACTU I enjoyed and was proud of the fact that I could work cooperatively with a variety of major corporations — such as Toyota, Sheraton, Heinz and Amcor — to deliver jobs for Australians. I would like to replicate at the local level what I was able to do at the national level.

As the member for Batman I am aware that this electorate has the largest Victorian urban constituency of indigenous Australians. I will work with my Aboriginal constituents to deliver to them the recognition that theirs was the original culture of this great land mass and as such deserves a special respect and recognition. Moreover, I will work with my Aboriginal constituents to deliver to them what I believe all my constituents want — equal rights to jobs, education, housing and health. That is what reconciliation is really all about.

The first duty I undertook as the member for Batman was to visit the graduates of a groundbreaking Aboriginal job training program in my electorate. The ceremony for the Aboriginal job training program was held at the Northcote Town Hall in my constituency where seventeen Aborigines graduated through a program run by a private indigenous company — Yuruga Enterprises. Fifteen of the seventeen graduates are now in permanent jobs.

It is my view, and it is a Labor view, that governments have a responsibility to intervene in the marketplace to give opportunities to all Australians to participate fully — and to participate equally — in our society. Working Nation was a marvellous example of a government program intervening to ensure that the benefits of economic growth in this country of ours are shared by all sections of the Australian community.

The people who now sit on the government benches have, despite their election rhetoric, in just a few short weeks shown that they have no real commitment to the have-nots. In fact the new Minister for Employment, Education, Training and Youth Affairs (Senator Vanstone) is ditching the very practical initiatives of Working Nation, and often for base ideological reasons. Just look at the way she abolished Nettforce, a primary example of a successful initiative which matched the needs of business to training programs.

The people who now sit on the government benches, in their election rhetoric, told the voters how they were a changed party, how they were now modern, soft and cuddly. They even boasted that their policies were now very similar to Labor's policies.

Have they really changed? We have now seen radio and television news broadcasts and newspaper headlines which take us back fifteen or twenty years. They are stories out of the early

1980s and the late 1970s. Go and compare the headlines. The news headlines talk about withdrawing rights to unemployment benefits. The 'dole bludger' tag is back as part of the rhetoric of government MPs. If you have any doubt about that, just go to the headlines of the Melbourne *Age* of September 1979. It says 'How Howard's axe fell on jobless'.

The morning news greets us with yet another Public Service bashing story — job cuts from the public sector, the slashing of government expenditure or the ripping away of more money from social welfare or job creation. It is done without any real consideration of the impact on families and on regional Australia. It is all about scapegoats for their own excesses.

Those election promises can be paid for only through their budget cutting processes. They are not really worried about reducing debt. They are worried about how they are going to pay for their own excesses. The truth is that, now that the Coalition think they are ensconced on the government benches, they have stopped the pretences which helped them win the election and they have started to revert to type.

Government ministers have taken out of their back pocket their real policies — Fightback, that ugly set of policies which were rejected by the people back in 1993. It is a tragedy that at the end of the twentieth century, when we should be going forward, we have a government which has put us into reverse and is trying to take us back to the late 1970s, the early 1980s or even the 1950s. It just cannot be done.

Australia has changed dramatically since those days. It is not the same inward looking country that we had in the late 1970s or early 1980s, when the conservatives last sat on the government benches. Just look at some of the basic indicators of those changes, and I am exceptionally proud of these indicators. Under the Fraser Liberal-National Party governments, the number of working days lost per 1000 employees due to industrial disputes was 591 days. Under the Hawke-Keating ALP governments, this had dropped to 194 days. In the early 1980s, our retention rates to Year 12 were abysmal — just over 35 per cent of the students stayed through to Year 12. Today that figure is well over 70 per cent staying to Year 12, and we should be trying to improve on that figure. But, unfortunately, the current government is not pre-pared to set targets.

If Australia is to take part in the Asia-Pacific economic revo-lution and the technological revolution, we must continue to expand on the educational opportunities available to our citizens. The most dramatic change in our workforce which the new gov-ernment must take into account is the increased rate of participa-tion of women in the workforce. Over the same period we have improved the social wage in this country to give our citizens not just services but quality services in the areas of education, health, social security, housing and community services.

When the Tories were last in government, only 13 per cent of GDP was spent on the social wage. Today we are past the 16 per cent mark, with specifically targeted and means-tested benefits. We have improved the rate at which the age pension is paid as a proportion of average weekly earnings from 22 per cent to over 25 per cent. Most importantly, we have dramatically improved the family payments for children, which are now also regularly indexed, as is the case with the pension, for increases in prices. Children's payments, as a proportion of the pension, with respect to those under 12, have gone from 11.8 per cent under the Tories to 16.6 per cent. For children between 13 and 15 years, they have increased from 11.8 per cent to 21.6 per cent.

I do not believe the Coalition can successfully turn all these advances back to replicate the late 1970s and early 1980s. The more they try, the quicker our side will be returned to the gov-ernment benches, because these advances are based on the essentially egalitarian political culture we have developed in Australia. Yes, there are hiccups on the way. Nothing is perfect. But at the end of the twentieth century, as we move into the next century, Australia can boast a political culture based on a sense of fair-mindedness, decency and equality.

Despite Labor's losses at the March election, I believe we still have basically a democratic-socialist political culture in this country. It is firmly based in the long struggles of the labour movement and will never successfully be completely rolled back by the conservatives. The more they try to roll it back, the more it will be at their own political cost.

None of this means that Labor can just sit and wait to be

returned to the government benches. The message from the Australian voters was clear: 'If you want us to continue to vote Labor, you had better rethink some of your key policy planks'. In an election in which the conservative wolves paraded as sheep, pretending their policies were similar to Labor's, we as a political force did not do enough to differentiate ourselves.

I am proud of the last thirteen years of Labor government, but I do not think that Labor did enough in the last election to show Australians that we understood. We had the policies in place to provide the stability and security voters demanded, to meet the challenges and the widespread concerns about the pace of change in this great country.

When my friends and I started out in the workforce in the early 1970s, there was a widespread expectation that, if I wanted, I could get a job and expect to stay with that employer, expect to stay in that same type of job, for the rest of my life, slowly progressing through the ranks. When my children start in the workforce early in the next century, they will have completely different expectations. They will probably stay with one employer for one or two years, maybe five years. They could be working from home and they will probably have several completely different careers, going back to educational institutions for retraining several times throughout their working lives.

It is these massive changes which are causing insecurity in our society. And it is not just in Australia. It is a phenomenon across the West ... that while the economics have started to boom, while there is real economic growth, it is not translating into jobs, not translating into opportunities for all sections of the community.

I am not going to pretend to give the prescription for this insecurity. I do not think anybody within the leadership groups of the labour movement should attempt any quick prescriptions. It is too early. We need to involve and consult with our grass-roots supporters in the party and the wider community. But I do believe we have to face up to the insecurity about the pace of change which played an important role in our defeat at the March election.

This should be the central issue of discussion and debate within the party over the next weeks and several months. How do we rebuild that sense of security? What is the role of government? Government, I believe, has an important role in providing the glue that sticks a society together. But the question is how governments should effectively intervene. How do they create that sense of security in an era in which real economic power has shifted from the nation-state to the multinational corporation?

If you feel secure about your job and the future of your workplace, it changes your outlook on the world. If you feel secure, you can start to feel secure about your relationships, your family, your neighbourhood and your community. If your job is secure, you feel less anxious about the future of your children's education. If your job is secure, you feel less anxious about your ability to find good housing. If your job is secure, you feel less anxious about your ability to get good health care. If your job is secure, you feel less anxious about how you will provide for your retirement.

In this debate about the creation of secure jobs, we need to find a way which is neither the European prescription nor the American prescription. The Europeans have delivered good full-time jobs for a few — but at the same time they seem to have accepted high levels of unemployment for many. The American model has substituted full-time, high wage, high skills, high benefit jobs with new part-time, low wage, low skills, poor conditions jobs.

We should not think we have new and viable policies to attract back the voters of Australia until we have gone out and visited the people in the cities and the regions. Only after a long and involved process of consultation will we start to come up with new and creative solutions to which we can get the broad commitment of the Australian people.

Nearly fifty years ago, Labor suffered a major electoral defeat federally. After that defeat we were out of government for far too long. I do not expect, under Kim Beazley's leadership, that will happen this time.

Chapter 8

Labor in the Future — Lots of Energy, Not Many Resources

Neil O'Keefe

It has been rare in recent years for us to be bouncing ideas off each other so openly. I think it represents a very healthy change from being bound so tightly by the strictures of office.

We should not try to compress this process too much. We have plenty of time to work through policy leading up to next year's ALP National Conference.

While there is the possibility of a double dissolution, that is more about raising funds and having candidates in place than hastily cobbling together 'a new vision for Labor'. If a double dissolution is called, the campaign will be about selling Telstra and the early poor performance of the Howard government.

One simple and obvious point should be made. We must have a general evaluation of our platform, philosophy and policies from the debates of the past. There will be no point turning up at the next election with the ideas the voters were looking for back then.

The agenda is moving too fast. The electorate is far more sophisticated. Already we have one million Internet subscribers in Australia. They will be wanting to know about our ideas for the future and they will be wanting to read them on their computer screens.

There is a need for a new policy approach for the next federal election campaign. In 1993 John Hewson tried the extensive policy route, 600 pages of it. It may have been the wrong policy — but Paul Keating cleaned him up with just one line — 'if you don't understand it, don't vote for it'.

This time round Howard made no serious commitment to policy apart from 'reforming' industrial relations and selling Telstra. Neither of those won him a single vote. The rest of his act was one of saying little about policy and concealing his true intentions.

Now I am not saying this is what we do, as it is not sufficient to rely on voter disenchantment with John Howard. Our movement has always produced ideas and we need to keep on doing so. Clear, simple concepts — yes. Volumes of detailed policy — no!

At present the ALP National Conference policy document runs to well over one hundred pages; in the section on resources and energy it is full of sops to every possible interest group — very few of whom campaigned or voted for us. This calls for a rethink.

It is vital that Labor presents itself in simple terms built around commonsense themes which can be refined down to a well understood sense of direction and purpose.

The more complex we make the manifesto, the harder this becomes. So I say to everyone who will participate in this process — keep it simple, keep it focused and, most of all, be prepared to have your key ideas fenced into a few major themes so that we go into battle fighting on as few fronts as possible.

Some themes reek of commonsense:

A fair and equitable living standard for all. Everything flows from this. The recent international reports on the wage gap and proportion of children in developed countries living below the poverty line presents Australia in a totally unacceptable light.

It is absurd that a country which is emerging as a key partner in the strongest growth region in the world, with the wealth opportunities that go with it, cannot find a way to ensure that the children of low-income and single-parent families have a decent opportunity in life.

Access to a quality job. Nothing will change under the John Howard equation. If anything it will worsen. We must be prepared to be more interventionist if we are to get the outcomes we are looking for.

Value adding. We must keep driving this on. There are still plenty of Australians prepared to vote for politicians who intervene to demand that businesses do more value adding and import replacement in Australia. We must be pro-active, we must lead.

Marshalling the huge power of our growing superannuation funds. Despite the fact that it is now nine years since Labor and the ACTU began this process very few Australians understand that there is now over $230 billion in our growing superannuation pool. Yet John Howard sold the concept that Australia was up to its neck in debt and that Labor was the cause of it. We did next to nothing to explain the magnitude and purpose of the capital base we have put in place.

Labor owns this one and it is up to us to explain it and to drive the funds to productive investment in the Australian economy.

Radical change to our tax system. It must be made simpler, fairer and much more transparent.

This is not a softening up for a GST. The Liberals own that one and they can have it. Nothing has changed since 1993 about the GST. There still is not one sensible economic, administrative or social argument for it in the Australian economy.

But that does not mean to say that the tax system is working well — clearly it is not. There are other ways to approach this. I have a few ideas and they will be put forward when the time is right.

However it is very important for us all to realise that talk of tax reform can easily become an Achilles' Heel for Labor at the next election.

The Liberals are saddled with their GST. No matter how much Howard and Costello deny it leading up to the next election they've got their mates out there talking it up and demanding it.

That is not a bad political formula for Labor as long as we do not fall into the trap of providing them with the chance to claim that 'Labor wants it too' — remember they were very successful in the recent election with the lie that 'Labor will sell Telstra too'. Do not think for one moment that John Howard would pass up the chance to misrepresent Labor policy on this.

So while the Fabian Society and the ALP cannot and should not avoid the tax debate — let us be very sure that there is no way we serve up a soft option for the conservatives with their GST.

Uranium and woodchips

The uranium industry describes the demise of the Federal Labor government as a 'window of opportunity' to strike while the iron is hot. The Liberals and Nationals are keen to accommodate them and about the only promise John Howard is keeping is the expansion of uranium mining.

They are moving quickly and it is possible that there will be several new mines operating in Australia when we come to office again. We have to think that one through.

The recent decision to lift the ceiling on woodchips comes as no surprise. The only thing that puzzles me are the protests of the conservation lobby. What did they think they were going to do?

Carmen Lawrence has made her view known from the environment side of the debate and I have done the same from this side. My point is, even if you thought there was some merit to the arguments about burning waste on the forest floor, there could not have been a sillier time to make such a decision.

It is only since Labor began phasing down export woodchips and restricting access to public forests that the industry has responded with substantial investment in plantations, private tree farming and more refined value adding.

Those pleading in 1983 for Australia to develop its own IKEA image would be thrilled to see some of the things now happening with high quality Australian timbers.

Three weeks ago I placed on the table, in a letter to the primary industry minister, an offer of bipartisan support to guarantee the Tasmanian pulp mill if they left the ceilings and the regional forest agreement process in place.

He chose to pass this up. Just when overseas investors were ready to invest here they have been given a very clear reverse signal. If they hang out long enough the Liberals and Nationals will revert to long-term guarantees of shiploads of cheap woodchips delivered anywhere they like.

My motto is, it is our timber, our plantations — if you want access to them then you invest in Australia. By the time John Howard gets a mill up here there will be no timber left to supply it!

Mining

We are going to have to do some thinking about the mining industry. Clearly, from what I am seeing around Australia, there are a number of very large projects on the drawing boards. They all claim to be Australia's most valuable project yet, sell themselves as a nirvana of export dollars and quote the number of jobs they will create. These projects are hugely seductive and it is easy to assume that sophisticated multinationals always get their sums right. They do not.

While supporting the industry through my portfolio activities, I am treating it with a healthy scepticism.

To start with, I make it clear that I am not about to help them through the difficult maze of native title negotiations and employment opportunities for traditional owners only to see them trying to pioneer Peter Reith style, non-union, individual contract sites.

I am not seduced by the notion of export income unless it really stacks up for the Australian economy. Issues such as Australian content in the supply of equipment and facilities and the source of capital have to be questioned.

There is nothing flash about a project which imports large lumps of expensive plant and equipment funded by huge amounts of offshore investment when the borrowings later turn up in the monthly outflow of the balance of payments.

Now that we have rebuilt heavy engineering and have our own capital I am all for buying back the farm — I expect to see plant, equipment and the capital sourced in Australia. This is not just a challenge to the industry. It is also a challenge to the superannuation fund managers and trustees. We have to make all the players aware that we want them working together to make it happen.

Energy and pollution

Finally can I sound one very significant warning about the energy and environment equation. Clearly, Senator Hill made a fool of himself by trying to position Australia outside the mainstream of world thinking on the greenhouse equation.

Without doubt industry will be forced to face up to the costs of energy and pollution post 2000.

The simple way for our trading partners to tackle this is to shuffle the deck so that first and second stage value adding — the major pollution and energy phases — are sent back to us.

It is already happening. In the past we were happy just to dig it up, load it onto a ship and let someone else do the dirty work of turning it into a useable metal. Now we are taking on the smelting; turning it into ingots and engine blocks.

We are hungry for the jobs and we are pleased to win the contracts. But if we are to take on this task it has to include the further stages up the jobs and value adding tree. None of us should be comfortable about being dealt just the energy and pollution hand — if we are going to carry the costs we need to earn the profits. These projects use up huge amounts of capital, energy and technology and do not create all that many jobs for the investment involved.

If we do not get more out of this then we have seriously to consider if it is worth carrying those pollution and energy costs for the rest of the world.

Now I think *we can win* out of this. We have a substantial natural advantage and we will advance up the value adding and jobs scale. That is the challenge before us if we are to turn opportunity into a long-term benefit for the nation.

I am very confident about the way we have pulled ourselves together as a national party; we are on the right track and Kim Beazley continues to grow in stature with his fine handling of his new role as Opposition leader.

We are right back where we started, relying on our own people for our ideas and drive — lots of energy, not many resources — but have no doubt will be there when it counts.

Chapter 9

Changing Labor, Changing Victoria: Labor's New Direction

John Brumby

I believe now, as I did on the day that I first joined the Labor Party, that gaining and retaining political power is the primary function of the Labor Party.

Gough Whitlam

I welcome the opportunity to contribute to this collection of essays aimed at the renewal and revitalisation of Labor.

It bodes well for Labor that so soon after federal and state elections, we can find the energy and the commitment to confront this challenge. To me, it is an affirmation that we are getting on with the job of moving forward — getting on with the job of rebuilding and renewal.

And getting on with the job of rebuilding and renewal means getting on with the job of regaining government.

When I joined the ALP in the mid-1970s I believed then as I do now that gaining political power is fundamental to implementing Labor's core beliefs and policies. It is a view put forcefully by Gough Whitlam in the 1960s. It is a belief which is shared and overwhelmingly supported by our party membership and supporters. Because without political power — without government — Labor cannot shape the future or deliver fairness and opportunity to all. That is why — if we are to win government and to govern well — we must embrace the culture of change and welcome the challenge of rebuilding and modernising Labor.

As I put it in a speech in May 1996:

> our challenge today is to put the Party's interest before per-
> sonal interest, to accept the magnitude of the task, to broaden
> the ALP and reach out into new communities, to renew our
> vision and policies for the next century and to find the
> resources and to raise the funds necessary to get the message
> to all Victorians.

And in meeting this challenge we must affirm and promote
Labor's enduring values and renew our policies so that they
properly reflect the needs and aspirations of a modern and rapidly changing Victoria. And perhaps most importantly, we must
engage the membership of the Party and the community gener-
ally in the process of debate and change.

Recognising the challenges

As a first step, we must recognise the dimension of the challenge
and accept the need for change.

At the heart of the state election result is a paradox. Nearly
half of this state wants us to be in government. And this in a
state in which Labor has governed for fewer than fifteen years
out of the last fifty and has polled more than 50 per cent of the
primary vote only twice.

Against this back-drop, Labor experienced a net gain of just
two seats. Despite the strong swing to Labor overall, we did not
poll well in the rapidly growing outer metropolitan areas, particularly in those seats in the east and south-east of Melbourne,
in those areas we need to win if we are to return to government.

And if we are to renew, to rebuild, to regain, we — the
Labor Party — must understand this paradox. While a review of
the results is in progress and no-one can claim to have all the
answers, some elements are clear.

Victorian voters, particularly in the east and the south-east are
yet to regain their trust in Labor. While worried by many elements
of the Kennett style — that he has gone too far — these voters
were unable to put their faith in Labor because we have yet to
convince them of our capacity to govern and to govern well.

And if we are to regain their trust, to embrace the future, we
must first deal with our past. The ALP has a rich history —

some good, some bad. We must acknowledge the past — the good and the bad — but we must learn from it, not dwell in it .

And fundamental to this is the need for a strong and rigorous set of financial principles to set the parameters of future economic management under a Labor government. Labor's Financial Management Policy commits Labor to a healthy recurrent budget surplus, a cap on debt as a proportion of gross state product, and appropriate bench-marking of all new spending outlays. It provides the basis for strong and sustainable economic growth. It is essential the public understands that our commitment to sound financial management and to the budget surplus is unequivocal and not negotiable. Without this we will be unable to regain the trust and confidence of the Victorian people, so essential to electoral success. This brings me to the second step, the need to build and renew around the base of Labor's core values and beliefs.

Labor values

The process of rebuilding begins with a solid foundation. That foundation is already in place. That foundation is Labor's core values. While Labor can lay claim to literally dozens of basic values, I want to focus on three which I believe are crucial to the process of renewal.

First, fairness, opportunity and prosperity. Labor stands for a prosperous, fair and creative society, rich in opportunities for all its citizens. But we also stand unambiguously and unashamedly for the underdog — united in our commitment to fight disadvantage and inequality, to protect the vulnerable and support those most in need.

The values of a fair go for all, a just and democratic society which believes in the right of every individual to reach his or her full potential, regardless of social, economic or geographic background. A society which equally values the corresponding right of every individual to dignity, security and respect.

Labor is the party, among all the other political parties, which believes in providing the opportunities in life, so that every individual can go on and achieve his or her potential. Only one political party does that, only one political party is absolutely committed to providing the foundations in life, through equality of opportunity, for people to go on and achieve success. That party is Labor.

Second, for change, reform and new ideas. And if you believe in these great Labor values as I do, then you will also know that Labor stands for change. I joined the Labor Party — and virtually everyone I know who joined the Labor Party — because it is the party of reform; because it is the party that is prepared to embrace new ideas.

If we stand still — if our policies relate to the past, more than they do the future — I do not think we fit the bill of being the party of ideas. We do not fit the bill of being the Party of reform and we do not meet the challenge of winning government and governing well.

Labor throughout its history has often had to re-examine long-held ideas and beliefs to move with the times. And it has done that in many ways including, of course, the most dramatic shift — the abandonment of the White Australia Policy. So we find ourselves today, through Labor policies, the most successful multicultural nation in the world.

This has only occurred because Labor has been prepared to embrace the challenge of change and to do what is best for the community.

Moreover, we have been more than just a willing partner in the process of change. It is Labor which has led community debate on the crucial issues shaping modern society — internationalisation and trade, technology and communications, and the meaning and impact of changing work patterns, class structure and gender roles on our society and economy.

Labor has been at the forefront in identifying changes affecting us all and our place in the world. And it is Labor which has been prepared to debate these issues and translate them into policies and action.

We must continue to take a leading role in change and reform. But in so doing, we must take the community with us. We cannot simply lead and expect others will follow. The process of change must be inclusive of the party and of the community as a whole. We must demonstrate Labor's deep commitment to social cohesion.

Third, inclusiveness and social cohesion. Labor also recognises that inclusiveness and social cohesion are essential to achieve progress and meaningful change.

We recognise that cultural diversity and tolerance strengthen, not weaken, the foundations of modern society and that the challenges we face can best be faced with more democracy not less.

As Prime Minister Hawke put it succinctly in his 1987 policy speech:

> the legitimate aspirations of the diverse groups and interests which go to make up the nation can best be achieved, not by fighting each other, not by setting group against group, Australians against Australians, but by working together, recognising and respecting each others' rights, fair expectations and fair hopes and aspirations.

So, Labor must continue to lead the process of change, but in doing so it must take the community with it — it cannot simply lead and expect or demand that others will follow. The process of change must be inclusive, not only of the party, but of the community as a whole. And it must be built on the core values outlined.

Let us turn now to the way forward for Labor in Victoria.

The way forward: Labor — a party of change and a party for change

Now is the time to remind ourselves and the public what the Labor Party is for as distinct from what it is against.

Labor is the party of the great social advances — these are the things that our party does so well: gathering up the instincts and impulses of decent people, gathering them up and turning them into policy. Turning them into things that take the shackles off ordinary lives, that let people be the best they can. These are the things we are good at. These are the things people look to us to do.

And these things can only be done if we are brave enough to continue to embrace change — to understand the world has changed and keeps changing, that Labor itself needs to change and that Labor has positive policies to change Victoria and

Australia. We will not succeed if we allow ourselves to become the party that stands still, that stands for oppositionalism, for saying no.

In that regard the state parliamentary Labor Party has taken the first steps in accepting the challenge of change and in particular the challenge posed by policy renewal. Our policy on drug law reform puts us at the forefront of progressive social policy in Australia. The decision taken on the question of the Grand Prix at Albert Park was a hard decision but the right decision. And now the party overall will engage in the process of debate and review with the aim of developing new, leading-edge policies for Labor. The media when reporting these first steps have characterised the debate as one of conflict and recrimination. To do so is fundamentally to misunderstand the debate.

I have asked the party to put oppositionalism and marginalism behind us. I have asked the party to understand that Victoria is changing and to embrace the challenge of developing policies which show we stand for change and which speak to the majority of the Victorian people. As leader of the party I have a responsibility to put issues forward, to make sure we have an open and far-reaching debate, to make sure every member right across the state has an opportunity to have a say in renewing Labor's policies.

I have announced the New Directions for Labor program, which will involve a series of monthly seminars on key policy issues, to ensure that all party members have the opportunity to be involved in fashioning the leading-edge policies that will win us the battle of ideas for 1999 and beyond.

Since the election, I have spent an average of two nights a week visiting branches, speaking with and listening to rank and file party members. Those members are hungry for a say in policy development and I am determined to make sure they are given a say, that the process of policy development is truly driven by the broader membership, that it is not captured by particular sectional groups or interests. And I am also determined to make sure the policies reflect the needs and aspirations of the Victorian community overall.

We must harness the goodwill and diligence of people in all spheres of life in Victoria. Government cannot be built on a combination of the so-called 'traditional' and minority groups alone. If Labor is to return to government we have to relate to and draw support from a wide cross-section of the Victorian community, including people whose upward social mobility, increased expectations and extended horizons are largely the result of opportunities afforded them by the labour movement in the past.

These are our people and we should welcome their advances and be seen to do so. We should understand that the great Labor tradition of looking after those most vulnerable and in need — a tradition which we uphold and will always carry with us — does not mean that Labor spurns those who have succeeded. While providing a social safety net will always be a major plank of our platform, our policy must also speak to and capture the aspirations of working people who enjoy a measure of success and rightly yearn for more.

We need to understand that success and a fair go can happen together. And if we truly understand that, much in the same way as Tony Blair has done in Britain, we will build the Labor Party into a party which leads the way ahead, that leads from the centre but is radical in the changes and opportunities it offers.

The modern Labor Party must be neither Old Left nor New Right, as neither remotely resembles the challenges ahead or offers a new way forward — a new direction for Labor. Our policies must reflect this new direction, and be built on Labor's core values for fairness, opportunity and social cohesiveness. And in the process of renewing our policies, we must also rebuild our party — its membership and its links with the community. There is no point in shouting our message from the rooftops of the inner city — we have be out in the outer metropolitan and provincial areas, being a part of those communities, listening to them and developing policies and initiatives which address their needs.

Central to this process is the Labor Listens program. Labor Listens will involve taking me, taking the Shadow Cabinet out into the community, strengthening community links in a formal way over the next 18 months. Labor Listens recognises that we must grow as Melbourne and Victoria have grown. We must renew our voice and contribute to the new and growing communities in this state.

We must attract the great silent membership which is out there in the community. At the Autumn State Conference I announced the *New Believers* initiative. I've set a target of 2 000 new party members to be achieved over the next 18 months, and I want to see those members become active members in the outer metropolitan and provincial areas.

So, we have started this process of Renewing, Rebuilding and Regaining now — as we must. We cannot simply wait until the next election is upon us and say to the people of Victoria — 'Here we are, new and improved — try us on for size'. We must regain their confidence and support over time. We must do the hard work now. We must be honest with ourselves and with the Victorian people. We must change ourselves and our party. And if we do, I know that the many, many Victorians who are thinking Labor but voting Liberal will return. All the instincts pull them towards us. Our job, right now, is to give them the confidence to put their votes where there hearts are.

The parliamentary party understands this and has embraced this need for change — this New Direction for Labor. Now every member of the party must embrace it too. To ensure this occurs, I will be meeting over the coming months with each of the policy committees to discuss and identify new directions for change. I will also be writing personally to each and every rank and file party member — inviting them to play a part in Labor's New Direction.

If they accept this invitation, if they respond to this challenge, then I believe a renewed Labor Party will meet the challenges of a changing Victoria — guided by its enduring aim of delivering prosperity, fairness and opportunity for all through socially and economically responsible government.

Index